WORDS

Pocket Guide to
SCOTTISH
WORDS

Iseabail Macleod

SCARAMOUCHE

First published 1986
by Richard Drew Publishing

This edition published 1998 by
SCARAMOUCHE, Glasgow G63 0RP

Copyright © Iseabail Macleod 1998

A CIP catalogue record for this book
is available from the British Liibrary
ISBN 1 899471 01 4

Designed by James Murray

Printed and bound in Great Britain

CONTENTS

INTRODUCTION

THE PURPOSE of this little book is to help tourists and newcomers to Scotland to understand some of the unfamiliar words, phrases and names they may meet north of the Border. It includes Scots words, Gaelic words, place-name *elements* (where necessary referring back to the Scots and Gaelic sections), personal names and a list of Scottish food and drink terms.

In a book of this size it is not possible to give more than a very brief introduction to all these subjects, but for those who would like to know more, a book list is provided on p. 88.

Many people find the language situation in Scotland confusing. What is the Scots language? Who speaks Scotland's other language, Gaelic?

Briefly, the Scots language comes from the same source as English, ie Old English, being descended from a Northern form of it. During the Middle Ages it spread from its original home in south-east Scotland to the south-west and right up the east coast. It diverged from the language south of the Border and by 1500 it was well on the way to becoming a separate language. Since the 16th century, mainly due to certain historical events, it has once more drawn closer to Southern varieties of English, but still retains many distinctive features. (For further information, see *The Concise Scots Dictionary*, Introduction, section 1.)

Gaelic is the Celtic language which the Scots brought to this country from Ireland about the 3rd century. By the 11th century it was spoken throughout most of what is now Scotland, but from the time of King Malcolm Canmore (1031-93) and his English Queen, Margaret, it ceased to be the language of the Scottish court. From that time the proportion of speakers in the population gradually dwindled over the centuries until today it is spoken only by about 80 000 people, and as an everyday language, virtually only in the Western Isles. (For more information, see *Why Gaelic Matters* by Derick Thomson, Saltire Pamphlets No. 5.)

Note that words in bold type in definitions are explained elsewhere in the book.

Note on place-names (see p. 63).

When looking for the meaning of a place-name, look up its component parts. As well as the place-name section itself, try the Gaelic and Scots sections where words and spellings still in common use are to be found.

Notes on pronunciation

The pronunciation key set out below, with no special symbols except for the vowel in th*e*, can be used to reach *something like* the sounds of either Scots or Gaelic. This does not mean that Scots and Gaelic have the same sounds, nor yet that either has the same sounds as those represented by the same letters in Southern English. Far from it, but if you use the key carefully, you will at least be able to understand and to be understood.

It should also be remembered that the pronunciation of both languages varies from area to area and in a book of this kind there is only space for one variety.

The following is a list of the letters used; note that
: indicates a long vowel. Stressed syllables are printed
in bold type.

Vowels

ə	as in	the, father
a	as in	pat
a:	as in	father
ay	as in	pay
e	as in	fed
ee	as in	week
i	as in	sit
Y	as in	bY
o	as in	lot
u	as in	hut
oa	as in	throat
oo	as in	school
aw	as in	bawl
ow	as in	fowl
a-oo	approximately the same sound as *ow* above, but longer	
oy	as in	boy
oe:	approximately as in French *oeufs* or German *Goethe*	

Consonants

Most consonants used in the key have *roughly* the same
sound as they have in English, but note: s as in see; g as
in get.

in Scots and Gaelic:
    ch as in German *Bach* and *ich*
in Gaelic only:
    gh pronounced similarly to ch, but voiced (ie
using the vocal chords)

^y a very slight y sound (as in English yes) at the end of a word.

b, d, g, are sometimes transcribed as p, t, k, but the actual sound is somewhere in between the sounds of these letters in English.

There are three ways of pronouncing l in Gaelic and many other points could be made. There is no space here, but if you would like to know more, consult the book list on p. 88, in particular *Teach Yourself Gaelic*, or better still, the records or tapes of *Can Seo*.

SCOTS — ENGLISH

MANY PEOPLE regard Scots as simply some kind of quaint dialect made up of words like *hoots mon* (which few Scots have ever heard off the English music hall stage). But the Scots language contains words and phrases at all levels, including even formal language, as well as words which all Scots use, sometimes without even realizing they are Scottish.

One interesting category is legal language. Though mainly derived from Latin these words are no less Scottish for that, the Scottish legal system being quite different from the English. Like education and the church, it was one aspect of Scottish life which remained distinct from England after the Union of the Parliaments in 1707. A few of the commoner legal terms are included in this brief list.

a [aw, a] all. **a body** everybody.

academy name given to many Scottish secondary schools, eg *Leith Academy*.

ach expression of disgust, contempt etc.

advocate in the Scots legal system, the equivalent of a barrister.

ae [ay] one; a.

agley [əglÏ] awry; wrong.

ain own.

aince once

airt a compass point; a direction.

11

alane alone.

ane, *(mainly East)* **yin,** *(mainly West)* **wan** one.

arbiter *law* an arbitrator.

ashet an oval serving dish.

astragal a window bar.

auld old. **Auld Lang Syne** long ago.

avizandum *law:* **ad avizandum** for further consideration.

awa away, gone left.

ay always.

aye yes.

bachle, bauchle [bachəl, bawchəl] an old worn shoe or slipper; a (small) uncomely, worn-out, untidy-looking person: *a wee bachle.*

back: at the back of five just after five. **the back end** late autumn.

bahookie *informal* the backside.

bailie *(till 1975)* a magistrate.

bairn *(mainly East)* a child.

Balmoral a kind of flat cap with a pompon on top and two ribbons behind, worn with Highland dress.

bannock a kind of round flat cake, often of oatmeal, but thicker and softer than an oatcake.

bap a kind of soft bread roll.

baronial of a style of architecture with crow-step gables, many small turrets etc, often seen on 19th-century mansions.

bawbee a halfpenny. **bawbees** money.

beadle a church officer.

beast a creature of any kind, a farm animal.

belt: the belt = **the tawse.**

ben (the hoose) in or to another room of a house,

usually the best room.

besom [bizəm] an unpleasant woman or girl.

better recovered from an illness.

bide to stay, live; to tolerate.

bield protection; (a place of) shelter.

big to build. **biggin** a building.

bing a slag heap.

birk a birch tree.

birl to turn or whirl round rapidly.

blaeberry the bilberry, a small blue fruit found on moorland.

blate shy, timid, backward.

blether to talk too much (about nothing or about something untrue). *noun* a person who does this; a talk (about nothing). **blethers** foolish talk, nonsense.

boiling a boiled sweet.

bonny lovely, pretty; handsome. **a bonny penny** a large amount of money.

bothy a rough hut used by shepherds, fishermen, mountaineers etc; accommodation for unmarried male farmworkers. **bothy ballad** a song (as) sung by such farmworkers.

brae a steep slope; a bank (of a river etc); a hillside.

braid broad.

bramble the blackberry *(fruit as well as bush)*.

braw handsome, fine-looking; excellent, fine.

bree juice, liquid, especially that in which something has been cooked or soaked. **barley bree** whisky.

breeks trousers.

bridie, *also* **Forfar bridie** a kind of meat turnover.

brig a bridge.

brither a brother.

broch a circular prehistoric stone fort.

brose a mixture of meal, usually oatmeal, and boiling water, eaten with butter etc.

broth a thick meat and vegetable soup (see also **Scots**).

bucket a rubbish bin.

burgh *(till 1975)* a borough, a town with a corporation.

burn a stream, small river.

Burns Supper a celebration of the birthday of Robert Burns, usually a dinner with speeches and songs.

but and ben a two-roomed cottage.

butterie *(mainly or originally North-East)* a rich bread roll, made with butter.

byre a cowshed.

ca [kaw, ka] to call; to drive; to set in motion (eg a skipping rope).

caber a large pole, tossed as a sport in Highland Games.

cairn a heap of stones, used eg as a marker or as a memorial.

cairry-oot food or drink bought for consumption elsewhere.

Candlemas 2 February, one of the Scottish quarter days.

canny careful, cautious; sparing; gentle, quiet. **no canny** unnatural.

capercailzie [kaypərkeli] a very large bird of the grouse family, the wood grouse.

carfuffle a fuss, muddle, confusion.

carl a man, especially a peasant or working-class one.

carline an old woman.

carnaptious bad-tempered.

cauld cold.

causey a roadway, pavement, especially if cobbled.

ceilidh see *Gaelic* section.

champit mashed.

chanter the melody pipe of the bagpipe; a separate pipe for practising.

chanty a chamberpot.

chaumer a room, chamber.

chiel(d) a young man; a child.

Church of Scotland the established Presbyterian church in Scotland, also known as **the Kirk. church officer** a person who is employed to carry out certain duties in a church, a sexton.

claes clothes.

clamjamfry a crowd, rabble.

clan a family group, especially one originating in the Highlands or Borders.

clap to pat (eg an animal).

clarsach the small Highland harp (see *Gaelic* section).

clarty dirty, sticky.

claymore *originally* a large two-handed sword used by Highlanders in the Middle Ages; *later* also used to refer to a basket-hilted broadsword.

cleg a horsefly.

cloot a piece of cloth. **cloots** clothing. **clootie dumpling** a **dumpling** boiled in a cloth.

close *(East)* a narrow passageway, especially a covered one between buildings; *(West)* the passageway entrance into a **tenement.**

clype *noun* a teller of tales. *verb* to tell tales.

cock-a-leekie chicken and leek soup.

college; the college the university.

Common Riding the **Riding of the Marches** in certain towns.

cone an ice-cream cornet.

convener a president, chairman.

coo a cow.

cookie a kind of plain round bun (see food section).

coorie: coorie doon to crouch down.

Corbett a mountain in Scotland of between 2500 and 3000 feet (761 and 914 metres).

corbie the raven; the crow; the rook.

corn in Scotland usually refers to oats.

corrie see place-name section.

coup [cowp] *noun* an overturning, a fall; a rubbish tip. *verb* to overturn; to capsize; to empty by upturning.

couthie pleasant; friendly; comfortable, neat.

Covenanter a supporter of the Presbyterian church in the 17th century.

crabbit bad-tempered.

craitur a creature, often used as a term of pity or contempt.

craw a crow.

creel a large basket for carrying peat, fish etc.

creesh grease, fat.

croft a smallholding, especially in the Highlands. **crofter** a holder of such.

crowdie *(in the Highlands)* a kind of rather crumbly soft cheese; *(in the North-East)* a mixture of oatmeal and water.

cruik [kr(y)ook] a crook; a hook.

cry to call, give a name to.

cuddy a horse; a donkey.

culpable homicide in Scots law manslaughter.

cundy a street gutter; the grating over it.

dae to do.

daft as well as English 'foolish, wild, crazy', means of low intelligence.

daftie a mentally subnormal person.

daith death.

deacon the president of one of the **Incorporated Trades** of a town. **Deacon Convener** the **deacon** who presides over the **Incorporated Trades** of a town.

deave to deafen; to bore, irritate with constant talk etc.

dee to die.

deer forest a large tract of (now usually treeless) land, originally reserved for deer-hunting.

defender in Scots law a defendant (now only in civil cases).

deid dead.

deif deaf.

deil devil.

deochandorous [dyochən dorəs] a drink as one leaves.

depute deputy *(usually after the noun)*: *headmaster depute*.

dicht *verb* to give a wipe or rub to, clean perfunctorily. *noun* a (quick) wipe, rub or wash.

ding to beat, strike. **go one's dinger** to do something or to act very vigorously.

dinna, dinnae do not.

dirk a short dagger, especially that worn in the belt as part of Highland dress.

dirl *verb* to (cause to) tingle, vibrate, ring. *noun* something which causes such; the sensation thus produced.

dispone to convey (land).

district *(since 1975)* a unit for local-government purposes, a division of a **region**.

divot turf, peat; a piece of turf.

dochter a daughter.

docken the dock plant.

dominie a schoolmaster.

doo a dove, pigeon. **doocot** [dookət] a dovecote.

dook *verb* to duck; to bathe. *noun* a duck(ing); a bathe; a soaking. **dookin for aipples** the **Halloween** custom of trying to get hold of apples floating in a tub or basin with the teeth.

doon down. **doon the watter** down the river, used of the holiday resorts on the Clyde, popular in the early part of this century.

doot to doubt. *Also as noun:* **I hae ma doots.**

douce [doos] quiet, pleasant, respectable, neat, tidy.

dour [door] stern severe; stubborn; dull, humourless.

dram a drink of whisky (of whatever size).

drap drop.

dreep to drip; to descend from a wall etc by lowering oneself until hanging by the hands, and dropping from this position.

dreich [dreech] dull, dreary, bleak, boring.

dripping roast something which is a constant source of profit.

dross coal dust.

droukit [drookit] drenched, soaked.

drouth [drooth] thirst; a drunk, a heavy drinker. **drouthy** thirsty; overfond of drink.

drove road a track formerly used by drovers taking animals, especially cattle, to and from market.

drystane dyke a stone wall without mortar.

dub a pool, pond, especially a muddy one.

dumpling a rich boiled or steamed fruit pudding.

dunt (to give) a heavy dull blow (to).

dux the pupil who comes top in a school or class.

dwam a faint; a daydream, trance.

dyke a wall, especially of stone.

ee, *plural* **een** the eye.

efter after.

eident diligent, industrious.

elbuck the elbow.

elder a member of the governing body of a Presbyterian church, a member of the **Kirk Session.**

eneuch [inyooch] enough.

entry a passageway between buildings; an entrance to a building, especially to a block of flats.

ettle to intend, aim, attempt.

even on continuously.

expecting pregnant. *She's expecting in March.*

fa (1) to fall.

fa (2) see **wha.**

factor an estate manager, land agent.

fae, *(rather old-fashioned)* **frae** from.

fair complete(ly).

Fair: the (Glasgow) Fair the traditional Glasgow summer holiday in the last two weeks of July; the first weekend of this period, the Monday being observed as a public holiday; also in other towns (especially in the West), in different fortnights.

faither a father.

fank a sheepfold.

fankle *verb* to tangle. *Also as noun:* **in a fankle.**

far: I could see him far enough I wish he were not here.

farl a three-cornered piece of oatcake, scone etc, a quartering of a round.

fash annoy. **Dinna fash yersel.**

fause false.

faut a fault.

feart afraid. **feartie** a coward.

fecht fight.

fegs exclamation of surprise or emphasis.

feu in modern times, a form of landholding by which land is held in perpetuity from a superior under certain conditions. Formerly the most important of these was payment of a **feu duty** but feu duties are now being phased out.

Finnan haddie a kind of smoked haddock.

fire-raising arson.

first: Tuesday first next Tuesday (see **next**).

first-foot to be the first to visit a house in the New Year; this person is called a **first-foot** or **first-footer. to go first-footing** to visit friends early in the New Year, especially in its first few hours.

firth an estuary; a wide arm of the sea.

fiscal see **procurator fiscal.**

fit (1) see **whit.**

fit (2) a foot. **fitba** football.

fite *(North-East)* white.

flesher a butcher.

flit to remove, move house.

foo *North-East* how.

footer *verb* to mess about, fiddle, act or work aimlessly. *noun* a person who does this; an exasperating person; something awkward, which is more trouble than it is worth.

forby as well, in addition.

fore: to the fore still around, alive, in existence.

forenoon the morning.

forest see **deer forest.**

forkietail an earwig.

fou full; drunk: **fou as a puggie.**

founds foundations.

foust [foost] mould, mildew; a mouldy smell or appearance. **foustie** mouldy, musty, mildewy.

frae see **fae.**

Free Church originally, the church which broke away from the **Church of Scotland** in 1843; now, the minority of it which refused to unite with the United Presbyterian Church in 1900, often known colloquially as the **Wee Frees.**

furth forth; outside, beyond the boundaries or confines of: **furth of Scotland.**

fushionless without energy, strength, ability, spirit or enthusiasm; insipid, dull.

fussle *North-East* whistle.

fykie fussy, finicky; tricky, awkward to do.

gae to go. **gan, gaun** going.

gallus bold, cheeky, tough, wild.

galluses trouser braces.

gan see **gae.**

gang to go.

gar to make, cause to (see **grue**).

gas: put someone's gas at a peep to make someone feel small.

gate *(now mainly in street names)* a street: *Canongate, Eastgate.*

gaun see **gae.**

gean a wild cherry.

General Assembly the highest court of the **Church of**

Scotland and other Presbyterian churches.

general merchant a shopkeeper, owner of a general store.

gey very.

gie to give.

gigot a leg of lamb or mutton.

gillie someone who attends on a sportsman shooting or fishing on a Highland estate.

gin if (only).

ginger a fizzy soft drink of any flavour.

girdle a flat iron plate with a handle, for baking over an open fire or other direct heat.

girn to moan, complain, grumble.

glabber soft wet mud.

glaikit (very) stupid, foolish.

glaur soft sticky mud.

gleg smart, quick(-witted).

glen a (narrow) valley.

glengarry a kind of forage cap, usually with two ribbons at the back.

gloamin twilight, usually the evening twilight.

golach an earwig.

gowd gold.

gowk a cuckoo; a fool (see **huntegowk**).

graip a garden fork.

gralloch to remove the entrails of (a deer).

grannie a chimney cowl. **yer grannie** an expression of contempt or disbelief. *I think it's a comet. Comet yer grannie.*

green a piece of grassy ground around a house etc: **the back green.**

greet to cry, weep. **greetin teenie** a person who is always crying, moaning or complaining.

grieve an overseer of farmworkers.

grilse a young salmon which has only been to the sea once.

grue *noun* a feeling of utter horror. *verb* to feel utter horror or fear. **It gars me grue.**

guddle to catch (fish) with the hands under the stones of a river etc; to mess about. *noun* a mess, muddle. **in a guddle.**

guff (to give off) a strong unpleasant smell.

guid good.

guising: to go guisin (of children) to go round doors at **Halloween** offering to sing, recite etc in return for small gifts (especially apples or nuts) or money. **guiser** a child who does this; *Shetland* a member of one of the squads in the Up-Helly-A festival, held every January.

gyte mad, crazy.

haar a cold East Coast sea fog.

haddie a haddock.

hae to have.

haggis a dish made of chopped offal, onions, spices etc, usually boiled in a sheep's stomach.

haiver to talk nonsense. *Also as noun* **haivers.**

hame home.

handsel *noun* a gift to wish luck for something new. *verb* to celebrate something new (with such a gift).

harl (to) roughcast.

haud to hold; **haud yer wheesht.**

haugh a river meadow.

heid the head. **heidbanger** a very stupid, crazy person. **heid bummer** a boss, the most important person in an organization. **high heid yins** those in authority.

hen term of endearment to a girl or woman. **hen-toed** pigeon-toed.

hert the heart.

het (1) hot.

het (2) *(in children's games)* it. *You're het.*

heugh [hyooch] a steep cliff; a deep gorge or ravine.

High Court (of Justiciary) the highest criminal court in Scotland.

Higher a secondary school examination at the more advanced level; a certificate for such.

hing to hang.

hoast (to) cough.

Hogmanay New Year's Eve.

hoodie (craw) the hooded crow; the carrion crow.

hunkers: on one's hunkers squatting.

huntegowk an April Fool (trick).

hurdies the buttocks, hips.

hurl *noun* a ride or lift in a wheeled vehicle. *verb* to move, push, pull, in a wheeled vehicle.

ilk: that ilk the same place. **Moncreiffe of that ilk =** Moncreiffe of Moncreiffe; now also means kind, quality.

ilk(a) each, every.

Immortal Memory speech in honour of Robert Burns at a **Burns Supper.**

interdict a court order prohibiting something until the matter can be tried by a court; compare English *injunction.*

ither other.

jag a prickle; an injection, especially an inoculation. **jaggie** prickly.

jalouse [jəlooz] to suspect, guess.

janitor, *informally* **jannie** a caretaker, especially in a school.

Jessie an effeminate man.

Jimmie form of address to any man.

joiner a carpenter, worker in wood.

jouk to dodge, avoid.

justiciary see **High Court.**

keek peep.

keelie contemptuous term for a rough, tough man, especially a Glaswegian.

Kelvinside an over-refined, rather anglicized way of speaking (referring to a district of Glasgow).

ken to know.

kenspeckle easily noticed or recognised, conspicuous.

kilt a kind of knee-length skirt with pleats at the back, usually made of **tartan** and worn by men.

kirk a church. **the Kirk** the **Church of Scotland. kirk session** the lowest church court, administering the affairs of a congregation. **come into the body of the kirk** to come closer into a circle of people etc.

kist a chest, box, trunk; a coffin.

know a knoll, little hill.

kye cattle.

lad(die) a boy, youth, young man; a son; a boyfriend. **lad o pairts** a young man of great promise.

laich, laigh [laych] low.

laird a landowner, landlord.

laldie a beating. **gie it laldie** to do something with a great deal of vigour.

Lallans the Scots language, especially a literary variety used by writers since the second quarter of the twentieth century.

Lammas 1 August, one of the Scottish quarter days.

land *(often in street names)* a **tenement**: *Gladstone's Land.*

lang long.

lass(ie) a girl, young woman; a daughter; a girlfriend.

lat to let.

laverock the skylark.

leal loyal, faithful. **the land of the leal** heaven.

lee lie.

leet a list of candidates for a job. **long leet, short leet.**

licht light.

line an authorization, eg an account with a shop, a note from a doctor stating incapacity for work, a prescription.

links (1) a stretch of usually grassy ground, often sandy, near the seashore; a golf-course (originally one on such ground); now mainly in place-names.

links (2) a string of sausages etc: **a pound of links.**

lintie a linnet.

loch a lake; an arm of the sea.

loon(ie) *mainly North-East* a boy, lad, youth; a son.

Lord Advocate the chief law officer of the Crown in Scotland. **Lord High Commissioner** the representative of the monarch at the **General Assembly** of the **Church of Scotland.**

lowp leap, jump.

luckenbooth brooch a kind of heart-shaped silver brooch, formerly used as a love token or betrothal brooch; the **luckenbooths** were lockable stalls in the streets of old Scottish towns.

lug an ear.

lum a chimney. **lum-hat** a top-hat.

Lyon: Lord Lyon the chief herald in Scotland and head of the **Lyon Court.**

mac familiar way of addressing a man, especially one whose name is unknown.

Mackay [məkY] **the real Mackay** the real thing.

maindoor flat a ground-floor flat with a door directly onto the street.

mair more.

maist most.

maister a master; a schoolmaster; *(as title)* Mr.

mak to make. **makar** a poet, especially a medieval one.

man a husband; also **mon, min** a way of addressing a person, especially to express surprise, exasperation etc.

manse the house provided for a Presbyterian minister. **son** or **daughter of the manse** the son or daughter of a minister.

march a boundary.

Martinmas 11 November, one of the Scottish quarter days.

mask to infuse (tea).

maun must.

meal *often refers specifically to* oatmeal.

meat food in general (as well as flesh).

meikle see **muckle.**

Merry Dancers the northern lights, aurora borealis.

messages shopping, things bought. **go the messages** do the shopping.

midden a dung heap; a rubbish heap; a rubbish bin.

mill lade a channel of water to a mill.

mind to remember.

minister a clergyman in one of the Presbyterian churches.

minor in Scots law, a boy between 14 and 18, a girl between 12 and 18.

miss: miss oneself to miss something good by not being there.

mither a mother.

morn morning. **the morn's morn** tomorrow morning.

morning roll a soft bread roll.

Morningside an over-refined, rather anglicized way of speaking (referring to a district of Edinburgh).

moolie mouldy; decayed, worn; stingy, mean.

moss (a stretch of) moorland or boggy ground.

mou [moo] a mouth.

muckle, meikle big.

muir a moor.

Munro a mountain in Scotland of 3 000 feet (914.4 metres) or over.

Munro-bagging the practice of climbing these, aiming to climb them all.

na, nae not. **nae weel** ill.

nane none.

neb a bird's beak; a nose; a tip or point.

neep a turnip.

Neerday [nayrday] New Year('s Day); a gift or hospitality given at this time.

neuk [nyook] a nook; a corner; a point of land.

next: Tuesday next the next Tuesday but one (*compare* **first**).

nicht night.

Nick: Auld Nick name for the Devil.

nip to tingle, smart, sting.

no bad very good.

nocht nought, nothing.

noo now. **the noo** just now.

nor than.

nyaff term of contempt for a small, insignificant or nasty person.

o of.

och exclamation of sorrow, pain or annoyance.

ocht any.

onie any.

oo wool.

oor (1) our.

oor (2) an hour.

oose fluff.

or before.

Ordinary-grade or **O-grade** a secondary school examination at the less advanced level; a certificate for such.

orra odd, spare, occasional. **orraman** odd-job man.

outwith outside, beyond.

ower over.

oxter an armpit.

Paddy's market a very untidy place (from the Glasgow street-market).

pan bread bread baked in a pan or tin. Also **pan loaf. talk pan loaf** speak in an affected, over-anglicized way.

panel the prisoner at the bar.

pape derogatory name for a Roman Catholic.

park an enclosed piece of farm land, a field, a football pitch. **parkie** child's word for a park attendant.

parr a young salmon, just before the **smolt** stage.

parritch porridge. **back tae auld claes an parritch**

back to one's normal routine.

partan a crab. **partan bree** crab soup.

past: put past to put away for later use.

pauchle, pochle to cheat; to rig; to steal.

pawkie humorous in a quiet, shrewd, dry-witted way.

pech to pant, puff, breathe hard.

peedie *Orkney, Caithness* small.

peelie-wally pale and ill-looking.

peerie (1) *Shetland, Orkney* small.

peerie (2) a spinning top.

peever(s) hopscotch.

pend an arched passageway, especially into the back court of a building.

perjink neat, tidy; prim; fussy, over-exact.

pey pay.

pibroch the classical music of the Scottish bagpipe; a piece of this with a theme and variations.

pickle, puckle a grain; a small particle or amount.

piece a piece of bread with butter, jam etc; **a jeelie piece.**

pig an earthenware container, now especially a hot-water bottle.

pinkie the little finger.

pirn a bobbin, spool.

piskie familiar name for an Episcopalian.

pit to put.

plain bread bread baked in batches of **plain loaves,** which thus have a hard crust top and bottom and soft sides.

pled past tense of plead.

plook a pimple, boil.

plowter to mess about in water; to potter about idly.

plunk to play truant from (school).

pochle see **pauchle**.

poke a paper bag. **poly poke** a polythene bag.

policies the grounds round a large house.

pooch a pouch; a pocket.

presbytery a church court above the **kirk session**.

press a large cupboard, especially a wall cupboard.

procurator fiscal the public prosecutor in a **sheriff court**; he also carries out some of the duties of an English coroner.

Prod(die) derogatory name for a Protestant.

provost the equivalent of English mayor; since 1975 used only as courtesy title by some local authorities, especially as **Lord Provost** in Edinburgh, Glasgow, Aberdeen, Dundee and Perth; in the Scottish Episcopal Church, the clergyman in charge of a cathedral.

proven: not proven a verdict that the accused is probably guilty but that evidence is insufficient; he or she is then discharged unconditionally.

public room a room in a house which can be used for entertaining guests, ie a sitting room, dining room.

puckle see **pickle**.

pudding a kind of sausage made with a mixture of animal entrails, blood, oatmeal etc.

puddock a frog; a toad.

puir [poe:r, payr] poor.

pun(d) a pound (in weight or money).

pupil in Scots law, a boy under 14 or a girl under 12.

pursuer in Scots law, a person who brings an action in a civil case.

quaich a shallow two-handled drinking bowl, now usually of silver and used as a trophy etc.

quine, quinie *mainly North-East* a girl, lass; a daughter.

ragnail a piece of loose skin at the base of a fingernail.

rammy a (loud) disturbance, a rumpus.

rasp a raspberry.

rax to stretch; to sprain.

rector the head teacher of a secondary school; a clergyman in charge of a Scottish Episcopal congregation. **the (Lord) Rector** a university official, now a public figure elected by the students.

redd to clear (out), tidy (up).

reek smoke. **Auld Reekie** nickname for Edinburgh.

region *(since 1975)* one of the larger units of Scotland for local-government purposes, divided into **districts.**

reid red.

renaig to refuse to do something, shirk responsibility.

retiral retirement.

richt right.

Riding of the Marches an annual festival in certain towns, especially in the Borders, having its origin in the patrolling of the boundaries **(marches)** of the **burgh.**

rin run.

rone a roof gutter. **rone-pipe** the pipe which drains water from this.

roon round.

round steak a cut of beef from the hindquarter.

roup a sale or let by public auction.

rowie *(North-East)* a kind of rich flaky bread roll.

rump steak in Scotland, a cut of beef corresponding to English topside + silverside.

runkle wrinkle; crease, rumple.

sae so.

saft soft.

sair sore. **a sair fecht** a hard struggle.

sang a song.

sark a shirt.

Sassenach (an) English (person).

scaffie a refuse-collector.

scheme or **housing scheme** a local-authority housing estate.

Scots/Scotch/Scottish there is much confusion about the precise use of these words. Briefly, in general current usage in Scotland, **Scots** is usual, except when referring to national or official concepts, when **Scottish** is preferred *(Scottish politics, Scottish schools, but Scots law);* **Scotch** is used mainly to refer to items of food and drink. In addition to **Scotch (whisky),** examples include; **Scotch bun = black bun; Scotch broth** a thick vegetable soup made with mutton; **Scotch collops** thin slices of meat simmered in a sauce.

scrieve to write.

scunner *verb* to sicken; to disgust. *noun* a feeling of nausea or disgust; a thing which or person who causes this.

semmit a (man's) vest, undershirt.

session: Court of Session the highest civil court in Scotland.

sett the pattern of squares and stripes in a **tartan**.

sgian dubh see **skean dhu**.

shed *verb* to divide, separate. *noun* a parting in the hair.

shenachie see *Gaelic* **seannachaidh**.

sheriff (1) **(sheriff principal)** the chief judge of an area.

(2) a legal officer who can act as judge in most cases (both civil and criminal) in a **sheriff court.**

sheuch [shooch] a ditch, drain, trench; a street gutter.

shieling a summer pasture; a rough hut on this.

shilpit thin, starved- or ill-looking.

shinty a hockey-like game, played by men, mainly in the Highlands.

shoogle to shake, rock, be or make unsteady. **shoogly** unsteady.

shot a brief use of something: *Have a shot of my umbrella.*

sic so.

siller money.

skail to disperse, scatter, separate.

skean dhu, *Gaelic* **sgian dubh** (meaning 'black knife') a knife or dagger worn in the stocking as part of Highland dress.

skelf a splinter, especially in the skin.

skellie(-eyed) squint-eyed.

skelp to slap, smack, spank.

skite to slide, slither; to (cause to) go off at an angle or in an odd direction; to strike, knock sharply.

slaister *verb* to work or do something messily, especially in a liquid. *noun* a state of (wet) mess or muddle; a person in such a state.

slater a woodlouse.

sleekit smooth, sly, cunning, hypocritical.

slitter *verb* to do something messily and wetly. *noun* a wet mess; a messy person.

sma small. **(wee) sma hours** the very early hours of the morning.

smiddy a smithy.

smirr a light drizzle.

smolt, smowt a young salmon between the **parr** and **grilse** stages; **(smowt)** a small thing or person, especially a child.

sneck a catch, latch of a door etc.

snell *of wind etc* cold and biting.

snib a catch or small bolt for a door etc.

softie a soft floury bread roll with a dent in the middle.

sonsy healthily buxom, chubby, plumply attractive.

sort to mend, repair.

souch [sooch] a rushing or whizzing noise; a deep breath, a sigh. **keep a calm souch** to keep calm or quiet.

soutar [sootər] a cobbler, shoemaker.

spale-bone a shoulder cut of meat, blade-bone steak.

speir to ask (questions).

speug [spyug] a sparrow.

sporran a kind of purse or money-pouch worn in front of a kilt.

sprauchle, sprachle to move or climb clumsily and with effort.

spurtle a stick for stirring porridge etc.

stance a stopping place for vehicles, eg a taxi rank.

stane stone.

stank a street gutter; a grating over it.

stave to sprain (a joint).

stay to live, reside.

stishie see **stushie**.

stook a small number of sheaves set up to dry in a field.

stookie plaster (of Paris); a plaster cast (for a broken limb); a plaster statue etc. *Don't just stand there like a stookie.*

stot (1) bounce. **stottin** drunk.

stot (2) a young ox, bullock.

stovies a dish of stewed potatoes, onions etc.

stour [stoor] dust, especially when flying in the air.

stramash a disturbance, uproar.

stravaig to wander aimlessly; to go about a lot, enjoying oneself.

stushie, stishie a fuss, commotion.

supper: fish supper a piece of fried fish with chips bought in a fish-and-chip shop.

sweetie a sweet(meat). **sweetie-wife** a (gossipy) effeminate man.

sweir reluctant, unwilling, lazy.

swither to hesitate, dither, be uncertain what to do.

syboe a spring onion.

syne (1) then; since.

syne (2) to wash, rinse (perfunctorily).

synod a church court between the **presbytery** and the **General Assembly.**

syver a street-gutter; a grating over it.

tablet a kind of fudge, of a hard consistency.

tae (1) a toe.

tae (2) to; too.

tak to take.

tap top.

tapsalteerie upside down, in a muddle, confusion.

tartan a kind of woollen cloth with a pattern of checks and stripes; such a pattern. Different patterns are regarded as belonging to particular families, but there is very little historical justification for this.

tattie a potato. **tattie-bogle** a scarecrow.

tawse a leather strap with thongs formerly much used for punishing schoolchildren.

tea, *also* **high tea** a main evening meal consisting of one cooked course, followed by bread, cakes, etc and tea. **teabread** semi-sweet buns etc. **tea jenny** a person (of either sex) who drinks a lot of tea.

tenement a block of flats.

teuchter [tyoochtər] derogatory word for a Highlander.

thae those.

that so. *I was that tired.*

thirled bound by some tie of duty, habit, affection etc.

thole to tolerate, endure, put up with.

thon see **yon.**

thrapple the windpipe; the throat, gullet. **weet one's thrapple** to have a drink.

thraw to throw. **thrawn** stubborn, sullenly obstinate.

tile hat a top hat.

till to.

tinker a travelling trader, living in tents, caravans etc, some with gipsy blood, but many of them descended from outcast Highland clans.

tolbooth a town hall; a town jail (now used only of certain buildings which formerly served these purposes).

town house a town hall.

trades (holiday) the annual industrial summer holiday in certain towns in the East of Scotland, eg in Edinburgh, the first two weeks of July.

trauchled overburdened with work etc, harassed.

trews *originally* close-fitting, usually tartan trousers; *now* tartan trousers worn by some Scottish regiments; short tartan underpants worn under the kilt.

tryst *noun* an agreed meeting. *verb* to arrange a meeting.

tumshie a turnip; a fat vacant-looking person.

twa, twae two.

twal twelve.

tyne to lose.

uplift to pick up, collect (passengers, parcels, money etc).

upset price eg at an auction sale, one which the seller would accept.

upstanding: be upstanding to get to one's feet, eg to drink a toast.

wabbit tired out, feeling feeble.

wae woe.

wallie ornamental, porcelain, china. **wallies** false teeth. **wallie close** a tiled entry (considered upmarket, especially in Glasgow). **wallie dug** one of a pair of ornamental china dogs.

wan see **ane**.

wan- un-.

wauk(en) to wak(en).

waulk to full (cloth). **waulking song** a *Gaelic* song formerly sung by Hebridean women while doing this.

waur worse.

wean [wayn] *(mainly West)* a child.

wee small.

weel well.

weet wet. **weet the bairn's head** to drink a toast to a newborn baby.

wersh of food or drink *either* tasteless, insipid *or (in some areas)* sour, harsh, bitter.

wha, *North-East* **fa** who.

whan when.

whaur where.

wheech [hweech] to move (through the air) with a whizzing sound, or very rapidly or suddenly.

wheen: a wheen a few.

wheesht stop your noise, be quiet.

whigmaleerie a trifle, fanciful ornament.

whisky see p. 87.

whit, *North-East* **fit** whit. **whit (or fit) like** what kind of.

Whitsunday 15 May, one of the Scottish quarter days.

wi with.

wife, wifie a woman, now usually an older one.

wrang wrong.

wynd see place-name section.

yestreen yesterday (evening).

yett a gate.

yin see **ane.**

yon, thon that *(indicating something at a distance).*

yowe a ewe.

GAELIC-ENGLISH

GAELIC grammar is a complicated subject and it is impossible to deal with it here in any depth at all. If you would like to know more about it, please consult the book list on p. 90; probably the simplest explanations are in the BBC's *Can Seo*. The following brief notes may help a little in finding words in dictionaries and glossaries.

Gaelic words change in a number of ways to form the plural, feminine, genitive, dative and vocative case of nouns, past tense of verbs etc. Changes will be found at the beginning, at the end and also in the middle of a word. A common change at the beginning of a word is the insertion of *h* after a consonant and this alters the sound of the preceding letter (eg *bh* and *mh* are pronounced like English *v*, *ph* is pronounced *f*). Thus if you are looking for a word beginning with *bh*, *ch*, *dh*, *fh*, *gh*, *mh*, *ph*, *th*, look it up in the dictionary without the *h*.

Common plural forms include:

-an	as in	eilean,	plural	eileanan
-ichean	as in	bàta,	plural	bàtaichean
change of vowel	as in	bòrd,	plural	bùird

The definite article varies according to grammar and spelling, for example according to whether the word is masculine or feminine, singular or plural, and according to the first letter of the next word, eg:

masculine	**an cù**	the dog
	am balach	the boy
	a bhalaich	boy (*vocative case*, ie when talking to him)
	bàta a'bhalaich	the boy's boat

feminine	**a'chaileag**	the girl
	na caileig	of the girl
	na caileagan	the girls
	nan caileagan	of the girls

Gaelic spelling seems more complicated than it actually is, and it is in fact much more logical than English spelling. One reason for apparently unnecessary letters is the rule of 'broad to broad and narrow to narrow', ie a broad vowel (*a, o* or *u*) in one syllable must be balanced by a broad vowel in the syllable before or after it; likewise a narrow vowel (*e* or *i*) must be balanced by a narrow vowel. Thus in *uairean*, plural of *uair* (time, hour), the *e* is inserted to balance the *i* in the previous syllable.

abair [apir] to say.

abhainn [avan^y] a river.

acair [achkir] an anchor.

ach [ach] but.

achadh [achəgh] a field.

agus [aghəs] and.

aig [ayk, ek] on.

aimsir [aməshir] weather.

ainm [anam] a name.

air [ayr] on.

air ais [ayr ash] back(wards); ago.

air falbh [ayr faləv] away.

airgead [arəkyət] money.

àirigh [a:ree] a **shieling**, summer pasture.

airson [ayr son] for.

àite [a:tyə] a place.

Alba [alapə] Scotland.

allt [a-oolt] a stream, small river.

àm [a-oom] time.

aodann [oe:tan] a face.

aonach [oe:nach] a hill; a ridge; a moor.

aosda [oe:stə] ancient.

aran [aran] bread.

arbhar [aravər] corn.

àrd [a:rt] high.

as [as] from, out of.

athair [ahir] a father.

bad [bat] a clump, tuft; a place, spot.

bàgh [ba:gh] a bay.

baile [balə] a town, village.

bainne [banyə] milk.

balach [balach] a boy.

bàn [ba:n] white; fair.

banais [baneesh] a wedding.

ban-mhaighstir [banəvYshtyər] a mistress; Mrs.

banrigh [banree] a queen.

bàrd [ba:rt] a poet, bard.

bàrr [ba:r] the top of something; cream.

barrachd [barachk] more.

bàs [ba:s] death.

bata [batə] a stick.

bàta [ba:tə] a boat.

beag [bayk] small.

bealach [byalach] a mountain pass.

bean [ben] a woman; a wife.
beatha [behə] life.
beinn [bYn] a mountain, hill.
béist [baysht] a beast.
beith [be] a birch tree.
beò [byaw:] alive.
beul [beeəl] a mouth.
Beurla [bayrlə] English.
bha [va:] was, were.
bho [vo] from.
biadh [beeəgh] food.
Biobull [beeəpəl] the Bible.
blàr [bla:r] a plain, a battlefield.
blàth [bla:] warm.
bliadhna [bleeənə] a year. **Bliadhna Mhath Ur**
  [bleeənə va **oo:r**] Happy New Year.
bò [boa:], *plural* **bà** [ba:] a cow.
bochd [bochk] poor.
bodach [botach] an old man.
boidheach [**boy**-yach] beautiful.
boireannach [**bor**anach] a woman.
bòrd [bo:rt] a table.
bothan [bohan] a small (rough) hut; in the Island of
  Lewis, one for the illicit sale and consumption of
  liquor.
bradan [bratan] a salmon.
bratach [bratach] a flag, banner.
bràthair [**bra:**hir] a brother.
breac [brechk] *noun* a trout. *adjective* **speckled,
  spotted.**
breacan [brechkan] tartan.
briagha [breeə] beautiful.

briogais [**bree**kəsh] trousers.

brochan [**bro**chan] porridge, greul.

bròg [bro:k] a shoe.

brònach [**bro**:nach] sad.

bruach [**broo**ach] a bank (of a river etc); a slope; a border, edge.

buachaille [**boo**achal[y]] a shepherd, herdsman.

buidhe [**boo**-ee] yellow.

bun [boon] the bottom, base, foot; a rivermouth.

bùrn [boo:rn] water.

bùth [boo:] a shop.

cadal [**ka**tal] to sleep.

caileag [**ka**lak] a girl.

cailleach [**ka**lyach] an old woman.

càise [**ka**:shə] cheese.

caisteal [**kash**tyal] a castle.

càite [**ka**:tyə] where. **Càit'a bheil thu** [**ka**:tyə **vayl** oo] Where are you?

calltainn [**ka**-ooltan] a hazel tree.

caman [**ka**man] a **shinty** stick.

camas [**ka**məs] a bay.

can [kan] to say. **can seo** [kan **sho**] say this.

caol [koe:l] narrow.

caora [**koe**:rə] a sheep.

caorann [**koe**:ran] a rowan tree.

caraid [**ka**rat[y]] a friend.

càrn [ka:rn] a cairn, heap of stones.

cas (1) [kas] a foot, leg.

cas (2) [kas] steep.

ceann [**kya**-oon] a head. **ceann-suidhe** [**kya**-oon **soo**-ee] a chairman, president.

cearc [kyark] a hen.

ceàrr [kya:r] wrong; left-handed.

ceart [kyarst] right.

ceartas [**kyar**təs] justice.

céilidh [**kay:**lee] a social gathering; a concert.

ceithir [**kay**hir] four.

ceò [kyaw:] mist.

ceòl [kyaw:l] music.

ceud (1) [**kee**ət] a hundred.

ceud (2) [**kee**ət] first.

ceum [kay:m] a step.

ciamar [**kee**mər] how. **Ciamar a tha sibh?** [**kee**mər ə
ha: sheev] How are you?

cìr [kee:r] a comb.

ciste [**kee**shtyə] a box, chest; a coffin.

clach [klach] a stone.

clachan [**kla**chan] a village round a church.

cladach [**kla**tach] a shore.

clann [**kla**-oon] children.

clàr [kla:r] a record, disk.

clàrsach [**kla:r**sach] a harp.

clò [claw:] print; a printing press.

clo [claw:] cloth, tweed.

cnoc [krochk] a hill.

co [co] who? **Co tha sin?** [co ha **sheen**] Who is that?
Co as a tha sibh? [co as ə **ha:** sheev] Where are you
from?

co-dhiù [co**yoo:**] however, nevertheless; anyway.

coig [**koa**-ik] five.

coileach [**kil**yach] a cock.

coille [**kil**yə] a wood.

còinneach [**koa:**nyach] moss.

coirce [**kor**kə] oats.

coire [ko̱rə] a cauldron; a kettle; a hollow in mountains, often near the top of a hill, a **corrie**.

coma [koamə] indifferent. **coma co-dhiù** [koamə kə **yoo:**] couldn't care less.

comann [koamən] an association, society, committee. **An Comann Gàidhealach** [ən koamən **ga:ee-**alach] the Highland Association. **Comann na Gàidhlig** [koamən nə **ga:**leek] Association for Gaelic. **Comann Luchd Ionnsachaidh** [koamən loochk **yoon**sachee] Learners' Association.

comhairle [kawərlə] advice, counsel; a council. **Comhairle nan Eilean** [kawərlə nən **ay**lan] Western Isles Council. **Comhairle nan Sgoiltean Araich** [kawərlə nən **skYl**tyən **a:**reech] Association of Gaelic Nursery Schools and Playgroups.

còmhla [kaw:lə] together. **còmhla ri** [kaw:lə ree] with.

còrr [kaw:r] more. **còrr is** [kaw:r is] more than.

crann [kra-oon] a mast; a plough.

craobh [kroe:v] a tree.

creag [krayk] a rock.

cridhe [kreeə] the heart. **gràdh mo chridhe** [gra:gh mo chreeə] love of my heart.

crìoch [kree:əch] a boundary.

crodh [kroa] cattle.

croit [krawtʸ] a croft. **croitear** [krawtyər] a crofter.

crom [krowm] bent.

cruach [krooəch] a stack.

cruinn [kroe-een] round.

cù [koo:] a dog.

cuan [kooan] an ocean.

cuideachd [kootyachk] also.

cuine [koonyə] when?

cùl [koo:l] the back.

dà [da:] two.

dachaidh [dachee] home. **mo dhachaidh** [mo ghachee] my home.

da-chànanach [da: cha:nanach] bilingual.

dall [da-ool] blind.

damh [dav] a stag.

dàn [da:n] a poem, song.

danns [da-oons] dance.

darach [darach] an oak tree.

de (1) [dye] of.

dé (2) [dyay] what. **Dé tha sin?** [dyay ha **sheen**] What is that?

dé (3) : **an dé** [ən dyay] yesterday.

deagh [dyə:gh] good. (see **dùrachd**).

dealbh [dyaləv] a picture. **dealbh-chluich** [dyaləv chloe-eech] a play.

dean [dyeeən] to do, make.

dearbh: gu dearbh [goo dyarəv] indeed.

dearg [dyerek] red.

deas [dyes] south; right(-hand).

deich [dyaych] ten.

deidh: an deidh [ən dyay:] after.

deoch [dyoch] (a) drink.

dha [gha] to him.

dhi [ghee] to her.

dhomh [gho] to me.

dia [dyeeə] god.

Di-ardaoin [dyərdoe:n^y] Thursday.

Di-Ciadaoin [dyeekeeatyin^y] Wednesday.

Di-Dòmhnaich [dyeedaw:neech] Sunday.

Di-Haoine [dyeehoe:nyə] Friday.

Di-Luain [dyeelooan^y] Monday.

Di-Mairt [dyeema:rsht^y] Tuesday.

dìreach [dyee:rach] straight; exactly.

Di-Sathurna [dyeesahurnə] Saturday.

diugh: an diugh [ən dyoo] today.

do (1) [do] your (*singular*), **thy** (see **thu**).

do (2) [do] to.

dóbhran [daw:ran] an otter.

dòchas [daw:chəs] hope.

doire [dirə] a thicket, clump of trees.

dona [donə] bad, evil.

donn [down] brown.

dorch [dorəch] dark.

dorus [dorəs] a door.

dragh [drəgh] trouble.

dràsda: an dràsda [ən dra:stə] now.

droch [droch] bad.

drochaid [drochat^y] a bridge.

druim [droe-eem, drim] the back; a ridge.

dubh [doo] black.

duilich [dooleech] sorry.

dùin [doo:n^y] shut. **Dùin an dorus** [doo:n^y ən dorəs] Shut the door.

duine [dinyə] a man.

dùn [doo:n] a fort.

dùrachd: leis gach deagh dhùrachd [laysh gach dyə:gh ghoo:rachk] with every good wish.

dùthaich [doo:heech] a country.

e [e] he; him; it.

each [yach] a horse.

eadar [aytar] between.

eagal [aykəl] fear.

eaglais [ayklǝsh] a church.

eala [yalǝ] a swan.

ear [er] east.

earb [erǝp] a roe deer.

earrach [yarach] spring, the season.

easbuig [espik] a bishop.

eile [aylǝ] other.

eilean [aylan] an island.

eilid [aylit] a hind.

éirich [ay:reech] to rise.

eisd [aysht^y] to listen.

eòlas [yaw:lǝs] knowledge.

eòrna [yaw:rnǝ] barley.

eudail: m'eudail [may:tal^y] my darling (*often to a child*).

eun [ayn], *plural* **eòin** [yaw:n^y] a bird.

facal [fachkal] a word.

faclair [fachklir] a dictionary.

fada [fatǝ] long.

fàg [fa:k] to leave. **fàgail** [fa:kal^y] leaving.

fàilte [fa:ltyǝ] welcome.

faisg air [fashk ayr] near.

falbh [falǝv] to leave.

falt [falt] hair.

fann [fa-oon] weak.

faoileag [foe:lak] a seagull.

fàs (1) [fa:s] to grow.

fàs (2) [fa:s] empty, unoccupied, deserted.

fàsach [fa:sach] a deserted place, wilderness.

fasgach [faskach] sheltered, protected.

fear [fer] a man; (*when referring to a masculine person or thing*) one. **fear an taigh** [fer ǝn tY] the chairman of a social gathering such as a **ceilidh.**

feasgar [fayskər] evening. **feasgar math** [fayskər ma] good evening.

feòil [fyaw:lʲ] meat.

feòrag [fyaw:rak] a squirrel.

feum [faym] need.

feur [feeər] grass.

fiacail [feeəkalʲ] a tooth.

fichead [feechit] twenty.

fion [feeən] wine.

fionn [fyoon] white, pale-coloured.

fìor [feeər] true.

fitheach [feehach] a raven.

fliuch [flyooch] wet.

fo [fo] under.

foghlum [foa:ləm] learning, education.

foillsich [fYlsheech] to show, reveal; to make public; to publish.

fonn [fown] a tune.

fosgail [foaskalʲ] to open.

fraoch [froe:ch] heather.

fras [fras] a shower.

frìth [free:] a deer forest (see **deer forest** in Scots section).

fuar [fooar] cold.

fuaran [fooaran] a well.

fuil [foo:lʲ] blood.

furasda [fooərəstə] easy.

gabh [gav] to take, have.

gach [gach] each.

Gàidhlig [ga:leek] Gaelic.

Gàidheal [ga:ee-al] a Highlander, Gael.

Gàidhealach [ga:ee-alach] Highland.

Gàidhealteachd [ga:ee-altachk] Highlands.

gainmheach [ganəvyəch] sand.

gàire [ga:rə] a laugh.

gairm [girim] a call; a cockcrow.

Gall [gowl] a Lowlander.

Galltachd [gowltachk] the Lowlands.

gaol [goe:l] love.

gaoth [goe:] a wind.

gàradh [ga:rəgh] a garden.

garbh [garəv] rough.

geal [gyal] white.

geamhradh [gya-oorəgh] winter.

geàrr [gya:r] *adjective* short. *verb* to cut.

geug [gayk] a branch.

geur [gayr] sharp.

gille [geelyə] a boy, young man.

giùthas [gyoo:əs] a fir tree.

glas [glas] grey, greenish-grey, green.

glé [glay] very. **glé mhath** [glay va] very good.

gleann [glya-oon] a (narrow) valley, **glen**.

gob [goap] a beak.

gobha [goaə] a blacksmith.

gobhar [goaər] a goat.

goirid [giridy] short.

gòrach [gaw:rach] stupid, foolish.

gorm [gorəm] blue; (of grass, leaves etc) green.

gràdh [gra:] love.

grian [greeən] the sun.

gruamach [grooəmach] gloomy.

gu [goo] to. **gu dearbh** [goo dyarəv] indeed. **gu leòir** [goo lyaw:r] plenty. **gu math** [goo ma] well.

gun [goon] without.

guth [goo] a voice.

i [ee] she, her.

iad [eeət] they.

iar [eeər] west.

iasg [eeəsk] a fish.

iasgair [eeəskir] a fisherman.

ìm [ee:m] butter.

inneal [eenyal] a machine, engine, instrument.

innis (1) [eenish] *verb* to tell.

innis (2) [eenish] *noun* a meadow; an island.

iolair [yilər] an eagle.

is (1) [is] is are.

is (2) [is] and (*short for* **agus**).

isean [eeshan] a chicken.

lag (1) [lak] weak.

lag (2) [lak] a hollow.

làidir [**la:**tyir] strong.

laigh [lY] to lie (down).

làmh [la:v] a hand.

làn [la:n] full.

laogh [loegh] a calf.

làr [la:r] a floor.

làrach [**la:**rach] a site; a ruin.

latha [**la:**ə] a day.

le [le] with, belonging to; by.

leabaidh [**lye**pee] a bed.

leabhar [**lyo**aər] a book.

leac [lyechk] a flat stone, slab.

leanabh [**lye**nəv] a (small) child, a baby.

leathann [**lye**han] broad.

leig [lyayk] to let, allow.

leis [laysh] with (the), with him, with it.

leth [lye] half. **leth-uair** [lye ooər] half an hour.

leum [laym] (a) leap.

liath [lyeeə] grey, bluish-grey.

linn [lyeen] a century.

linne [lyeenə] a pool; a waterfall.

loch [loch] a loch, lake. **lochan** [lochan] a little loch.

lom [lowm] bare.

lòn (1) [law:n] food.

lòn (2) [law:n] a meadow, a marsh.

lon-dubh [lon doo] a blackbird.

long [long] a ship.

lorg [lorək] a track, trace.

luaidh: a luaidh [ə looa-ee] (my) darling.

luath [looə] fast, quick, swift.

lùb [loo:p] a bend.

luch [looch] a mouse.

luchd [loochk] people. **luchd-turuis** [loochk tooreesh] tourists.

lus [loos] a plant.

mac [machk] a son.

machair [machir] a low-lying fertile plain; a sandy field behind a beach.

madadh [matəgh] a dog; an animal of the dog family: **madadh-allaidh** [matəgh alee] a wolf; **madadh-ruadh** [matəgh rooəgh] a fox.

madainn [matanʸ] morning.

maighdean [mYtyən] a maiden.

maireach: am maireach [əma:rach] tomorrow.

maol [moe:l] bald, bare.

mar [mar, mər] as, like. **mar sinn** [mər sheen] like that.

marbh [marəv] dead.

math [ma] good. **'s math sin** [sma **sheen**] that's good.
màthair [**ma:**hir] a mother.
meadhon [**mee**ən] middle.
meall [**mya**-ool] a lump, heap; a rounded hill.
measg: am measg [əmaysk] among.
meur [may:r] a finger; a branch.
mi [mee] I, me.
mi- [mee] not, un-.
mil [meel] honey.
mìle [**mee:**lə] a thousand; a mile.
minisdear [**mee**neeshtyər] a minister.
mìos [mee:əs] a month.
mise [**mee**shə] I, me (*emphatic*).
mo [mo] my.
moch [moch] early.
mòd [maw:t] a festival of Gaelic song, music and poetry.
mòine [**maw:**nyə] peat.
monadh [**mo**nəgh] a hill, mountain; a range; a moor.
mór [moa:r] big.
móran [**moa:**ran] much, a lot, many.
muc [moochk] a pig.
muigh: am muigh [əmooee] outside.
muileann [**moo**lan] a mill.
muir [**moo**-eer] the sea.
mullach [**moo**lach] a summit, hilltop.
na [na, nə] the (*plural*); of the (*feminine*).
nach [nach] that . . . not; which . . . not; who . . . not.
naidheachd [**nY**achk] news.
nan [nən] of the (*plural*).
naoi [noe:ee] nine.
naomh [noe:v] a saint.
nead [net] a nest.

neo- [nyo] un-, not.

neo see **no**.

neònach [nyaw:nach] strange.

neul [nayl] a cloud.

nì [nyee:] will do, will make.

nighean [nyeeən] (*as part of name*) **nic** [nyeechk] a daughter.

nis: a nis [əneesh] now.

no, neo [no, nyo] or.

nochd (1) [nochk] a night.

nochd (2) [nochk] to show.

Nollaig [nolek] Christmas. **Nollaig chridheil** [nolek chreeəl] Merry Christmas.

nota [notə] a pound note.

nuadh [nooəgh] new.

nuair [nooər] when.

nuas: a nuas [ənooəs] down.

null: a null [ənool] over (to here).

o [o] from.

obair [oapər] work.

ochd [ochk] eight.

odhar [oər] dun-coloured, fawnish brown.

òg [aw:k] young.

oidhche [oe-eechə] a night.

oifis [ofeesh] an office. **oifis a' phuist** [ofeesh ə foosht^y] post office.

oilthigh [olhY] a university.

oir (1) [o-eer] for, because.

oir (2) [o-eer] an edge.

òl [aw:l] to drink.

ola [olə] oil.

olc [olək] evil.

ollamh [oləv] (*mainly in titles*) professor, (non-medical) doctor. *An t-Ollamh MacIain* Dr Johnson.

òr [aw:r] gold.

òraid [aw:rat^y] a speech.

òran [aw:ran] a song.

òrd [aw:rd] a hammer.

os cionn [os kyoo:n] above.

ospadal [ospatal] a hospital.

pàigh [pa:ee] to pay.

paipear [pa-eepər] paper. **paipear naidheachd** [pa-eepər na-eeyachk] a newspaper.

partan [parshtan] a crab.

pathadh [pahəgh] thirst.

peann [pya:oon] a pen.

piob [peeəp] a pipe.

piobaire [peeəpərə] a piper.

piobairachd [peeəpərachk] pipe music; pibroch (see **pibroch** in Scots section).

piob-mhór [peeəp voa:r] the bagpipe.

piuthar [pyooar] a sister.

pòg [paw:k] kiss.

poll [powl] a pool; a hole; mud; a muddy field.

port (1) [poarsht] a port; a landing place on the shore, cleared for small boats.

port (2) [poarsht] a tune. **port-a-beul** [poarsht ə beeəl] mouth-music.

pòs [paw:s] to marry. **pòsda** [paw:stə] married.

prìs [pree:sh] a price.

pùnnd [poo:nt] a pound (in weight or money).

raineach [ranyach] fern; bracken.

ràinig [ra:neek] reached.

rann [ra-oon] a verse.

raoir: an raoir [ən **roe**eer] last night.

rathad [**ra**ət] a road.

reamhar [**ra**-oor] fat.

reic [raychk] to sell.

reul [**ray**:l] a star.

ri [ree] to.

riamh [**ree**əv] ever.

ribhinn [**ree:**veenʸ] a maiden.

righ [ree:] a king.

rinn [rYn] made, did.

ris [reesh] to (the), to him, to it.

rithist: a rithist [əree-ishtʸ] again.

roimh [roy] before.

ròn [raw:n] a seal.

ros (1) [ros] a promontory.

ròs (2) [raw:s] a rose.

ruadh [**roo**əgh] red, brownish red, red-brown.

rubha [**roo**ə] a headland, promontory.

rud [root] a thing.

rugadh [**roo**kəgh] was born.

sabaid [**sa**patʸ] to fight, struggle.

Sàbaid [**sa:**patʸ] Sabbath. **latha na Sàbaid** [la: nəsa:patʸ] Sunday.

sagart [**sa**kart] a priest.

saighdear [**s**Ytyər] a soldier.

sàil [sa:lʸ] a heel.

salach [**sa**lach] dirty.

salann [**sa**lan] salt.

salm [**sa**ləm] a psalm.

sàmhach [**sa:**vach] quiet.

samhradh [**sa**-oorəgh] summer.

saor (1) [soe:r] a joiner, carpenter.

saor (2) [soe:r] free.

Sasunnach [sasənach] English; an Englishman.

seachd [shachk] seven.

seachdainn [shachkanʸ] a week.

seall [sha-ool] to look (at). **seall seo** [sha-ool sho] look at this.

sean [shen] old.

seanachaidh [shenachee] a teller of traditional Gaelic stories.

seanair [shenar] a grandfather.

seanmhar [shenevər] a grandmother.

seinn [shYn] to sing.

seirbhis [sherəveesh] service.

seo [sho] this. **an seo** [ən sho] here.

seòl [shaw:l] sail.

seòrsa [shaw:rsə] a kind, sort.

sgadan [skatan] a herring.

sgeilp [skayləp] a shelf.

sgeul [skay:l] a story.

sgian [skeeən] a knife.

sgiath [skeeə] a wing.

sgillinn [skeeleen] a penny.

sgith [skee:] tired.

sgoil [skolʸ] a school.

sgriobh [srkeeəv] to write.

sguab [skooəp] *noun* a sheaf; a brush, broom. *verb* to sweep.

sguir [skoor] to stop.

sia [sheeə] six.

sian [sheeən] a storm.

siar [sheeər] west(ern).

sibh [sheev] you (*plural and polite form — compare* vous *in*

French).

side [shee:tə] weather.

sin (1) [sheen] that. **an sin** [ən **sheen**] there.

sin (2) [shee:n] to stretch (out).

sionnach [**shee**ənəch] a fox.

siorrachd [**shi**rachk] a county, shire.

sìth [shee:] peace.

sìthiche [shee:heechə] a fairy.

siubhail [**shoo**alʸ] to travel.

siucar [**shooch**kar] sugar.

siud [shoot] that (*indicating something at a distance*).

slàinte [sla:ntyə] health. **slàinte mhath** [sla:ntyə va] good health (*as a toast*).

slàn [sla:n] healthy.

slaodach [**sloe**:tach] slow.

slat [slat] a rod.

slighe [shleeə] a path, way.

sliochd [shleeəchk] descendants.

sloc(hd) [slochk] a pit, hollow.

smeòrach [**smyaw**:rach] a thrush.

snàmh [sna:v] to swim.

sneachda [**shnyach**kə] snow.

snog [snok] nice, pretty.

soisgeul [**sos**gayl] gospel.

sòlas [**saw**:las] happiness, joy.

solus [**sol**əs] light.

sonas [**son**əs] happiness.

soraidh [**sor**ee] farewell.

spàin [spa:nʸ] a spoon.

spéis [spay:sh] affection, regard.

spiorad [**spee**rat] spirit.

spòg [spaw:k] a paw, claw.

sporan [sporan] a purse, **sporran** (see Scots section).

spréidh [spray:] cattle.

sràid [sra:t^y] a street.

sròn [sraw:n] a nose.

sruth [sroo] a steam.

stad [stat] stop.

staigh: a staigh [ə stY] in(side).

steach: a steach [ə styach] into.

steall [stya-ool] a gush, spout.

strùpag [stroo:pak] a cup of tea.

suas [sooəs] up.

suidh [sooee] to sit.

sùil [soo:l^y] an eye.

taigh [tY] a house. **taigh-osda** [tY aw:stə] a hotel.

talamh [talav] earth.

tana [tanə] thin.

taobh [toe:v] side. **ri taobh** [ree toe:v] beside.

tapadh leat [tapə let], (*plural and polite form — see*
   sibh) **tapadh leibh** [tapə lYv] thank you.

tarsainn [tarsan^y] across.

tasdan [tastan] a shilling.

té [tyay] a woman, (*when referring to a feminine person*
   or thing) one.

teagaisg [tyəkisk] to teach.

teagamh [tyəkəv] doubt.

teaghladh [tyəghləgh] a family.

teth [tye] hot.

tha [ha:] is, are, am.

thàinig [ha:neek] came.

thairis [hareesh] over, across.

thall [howl] (over) there. **thall's a bhos** [howl sə **vos**]
   here and there.

theid [hay:t^y] will come.

their [hayr] will say.

thoir [**ho**-eer] to give, take, bring.

thu [oo:] you (*familiar form — compare* tu *in French*).

thug [hook] gave, took, brought.

thubhairt [**hoo**irsht^y] said.

thusa [**oo**sə] you (*emphatic of familiar form*).

tì [tee] tea.

tighearna [**tyee**ərnə] lord.

till [tyee:l] to come back, return.

tioram [**tyee**rəm] dry.

tìr [tyee:r] land. **tìr-mór** [tyee:r **moa**:r] mainland.

tiugainn [**tyoo**keen^y] come.

tog [toak] to lift; to build.

toilichte [to**leech**tyə] pleased, happy.

toiseach [**to**shach] beginning.

tonn [town] a wave.

traigh [**tra**-ee] a shore.

trang [trang] busy.

tràth [tra:] early.

trì [tree:] three.

tric [treechk] often.

trom [trowm] heavy.

tuath [**too**ə] north.

tuathanach [**too**əhanəch] a farmer.

turus [**too**rəs] a journey.

uachdar [**oo**:əchkar] the top, upper part; cream.

uaine [**oo**:anyə] green.

uair [**oo**ər] an hour; time. **an uair** [ən **oo**ər] when. **Dé an uair a tha e?** [dyay ən **oo**ər ə ha: e] What time is it?

uamh [**oo**:av] a cave.

uamhasach [**oo**:avasach] awful(ly).

uan [ooan] a lamb.

uasal [ooasal] noble.

ubhal [oo-al] an apple.

ud [oot] that (*indicating something at a distance*).

ugh [oo] an egg.

ùghdaras [oo:tərəs] authority.

uile [oolə] every, all.

ùine [oo:nyə] time.

uinneag [oonyak] a window.

uiseag [ooshak] a lark.

uisge [ishkə] water. **uisge-beatha** [ishkə behə] whisky.

ullamh [oolav] ready.

ùr [oo:r] new.

ùrlar [oo:rlar] a floor; *in bagpipe music* the (main) theme of a **pibroch**.

ùrnuigh [oo:rənY] a prayer.

SCOTTISH PLACE-NAMES

SCOTTISH place-names come from many different sources. Some, especially river names, come from sources of which there is now no provable explanation, some possibly from languages which have left no other trace. But the most striking aspect of Scottish names is the large number which are of Gaelic origin, even in the south-eastern part of the country, which may never have been entirely Gaelic-speaking. Many of these names are obscured by strange spellings, owing to the fact that the majority of early mapmakers and other recorders were not familiar with Gaelic. They wrote the names down as they heard them, resulting in anglicized forms such as *Balmore* for *Bail(e) mór* (the big town or village). Alternatively, they read them in a genuine Gaelic source, pronounced these names according to English pronunciation and wrote down the result of that, eg *Gleneagles* for *Gleann Eaglais* (glen of the church).

Another rich source of place-names is Old Norse, especially names from the time of the Norse invasions of the West Coast from the 9th to the 13th century; these are found in abundance in the Western Isles (though in strongly Gaelicized form). In Shetland and Orkney, where Norse domination lasted longer, names are predominantly from this source, and fair numbers of Scandinavian names are found in other areas, especially in the South-West.

Older strata of names include the British of the pre-Roman inhabitants (a Celtic language related to modern Welsh and Breton) and English names brought north with the Angles from the 7th century on. The Picts, the mysterious people who inhabited Eastern Scotland north of the Forth from about the 3rd to the 9th century, have also left their mark on place-names; their language is believed to have been Celtic and the most prominent place-name element from it is *pit-*.

Many names from more recent centuries are of course from Scots or English words and are thus more easily recognizable. For further information, see book list on p. 92.

Two notes on Older Scots spelling may be helpful:
   z sometimes represents Older Scots ȝ, which was pronounced roughly like the *y* sound in English 'million'. In some names, e.g. *Lenzie*, the *z* is now pronounced as in English, but in others, e.g. *Dalrulzion* [dal**ril**yən], the old pronunciation is retained;
   quh- is an Older Scots form of *wh-*, as in *Balquhidder* [bal**whi**dər].

The following is a very brief list of common place-name elements, where necessary referring back to the Scots-English or Gaelic-English sections.

a *from Old Norse* **á** a river.
-a see **-ey**.
aber *Pictish* or *British* a rivermouth.
ach, auch [ach, och] from *Gaelic* achadh a field.
-aig often represents *Old Norse* **vík** a bay, as in *Arisaig* Ari's bay.
aird *Gaelic* = a height.

annat, annet from *Old Gaelic* **annaid** a church, mother church.

ardan, arden from *Gaelic* **àird** a height; a point of land; the ending is from *Gaelic* **an** meaning 'of the'.

auch see **ach.**

auchan, auchen [ochən] from *Gaelic* **achadh** a field; the ending is from *Gaelic* **an** meaning 'of the'.

auchter, ochter from *Gaelic* **uachdar** the surface, top; upper part.

ault [olt] from *Gaelic* **allt** a stream.

-ay see **-ey.**

bal, bally from *Gaelic* **baile** a town, village.

balloch, belloch from *Gaelic* **bealach** a mountain pass; but **Balloch** [baloch] near Inverness is **Bail' an Loch** the village on the loch.

ban(e) from *Gaelic* **bàn** white, light-coloured, fair.

bar(r) from *Gaelic* **bàrr** the top.

beg from *Gaelic* **beag** small.

belloch see **balloch.**

ben from *Gaelic* **beinn** a mountain, hill.

-bie, -by from *Old Norse* **býr** a farm, village.

blair from *Gaelic* **blàr** a field, a battlefield.

-bost, -bister, -bster, -busta, -boll, -poll, -pool are all reduced forms of *Old Norse* **bólstaðr** a farm, farmstead, homestead, dwelling place.

breck from *Gaelic* **breac** speckled, spotted; a trout.

bun *Gaelic* = the foot; a rivermouth.

-by see **-bie.**

caer *British* a fort.

cairn from *Gaelic* **càrn** a heap of stones.

calder a stream name from ancient *British* meaning 'hard water'.

cambus from *Gaelic* **camas** a bay.

car there are several possible sources, including *British* **caer**, a fort, *Gaelic* **càrn** a cairn, or **ceathramh** a fourth part, or **cathair** a town, a fort, or **càrr** a rock ledge.

carse *Scots* = a stretch of low-lying land along a river.

clash, cleish from *Gaelic* **clais** a furrow, groove, ditch.

cleugh [klyooch] *Scots* = a gorge, ravine.

close (*in street-names*) see Scots section.

coll, collie, colly from *Gaelic* **coille** a wood.

cool see **coul**.

corrie *Scots* spelling of *Gaelic* **coire** a hollow in mountains, especially one near the top of a hill.

cors(e) frequent *Scots* spelling variant(s) of 'cross'.

coul from *Gaelic* **cùl** the back.

craig, craik from *Gaelic* **creag** a rock, or in some cases from *British* **carreg.**

cro(e) from *Gaelic* **crodh** cattle.

dal(l), dail, dol, dul from the *British* word for a river meadow (in a valley); usually at the beginning of a name but very occasionally at the end, as in Cromdale; see **-dal(l)** below.

-dal(l), -dale, -dail from *Old Norse* **dalr,** a valley; always at the end of a name; see **dal(l)** above.

damph from *Gaelic* **damh** a stag.

darrach, darroch from *Gaelic* **darach** an oak tree.

dauch, dava(ch), doch from *Gaelic* **dabhach** a vat, tub; an old land measure (based on the amount of grain etc the land could yield).

dhu from *Gaelic* **dubh** black.

din from *Celtic*, meaning a fort: either *Welsh* **din** or *Gaelic* **dùn**.

doch see **dauch**.

dol see **dal(l)**.

doon, doun(e) often from *Gaelic* **dùn**, a fort.

drochit from *Gaelic* **drochaid** a bridge.

drom, drum from *Gaelic* **druim** the back; a ridge.

dul see **dal(l)**.

dum, dun from *Gaelic* **dùn** a fort.

eccles either from *Gaelic* **eaglais** or *Welsh* **eglwys** or directly from their origin, *Latin* **ecclesia,** all meaning church.

edin from *Gaelic* **aodann** a face.

enach, enoch from *Gaelic* **aonach** a hill; a ridge; a moor.

entry (*in street names*) see Scots section.

ess from *Gaelic* **eas** a waterfall.

-ey, -ay, -a *Old Norse* **ey** an island.

fal(l) often from *Older Scots, Middle English* **faw** variegated, of different colours.

fas often from *Old Gaelic* = a stance, a place to stop (eg for a night).

fauld Scots spelling of 'fold'.

fell from *Old Norse* **fell, fjall** a hill, mountain.

ferin from *Gaelic* **fearran** land; an estate, farm.

fern often from *Gaelic* **feàrna** an alder.

fin(n) from *Gaelic* **fionn** white, pale-coloured.

firth *Scots* = an estuary; a wide arm of the sea.

forest a **deer forest** (see Scots section).

gair, gare *Gaelic* **geàrr** short.

gart from *Irish* **gart, gort,** or *British* **garth** a field, enclosure, or *Old Norse* **garðr** an enclosure.

garv from *Gaelic* **garbh** rough.

gate *Scots* (*now mainly in street names*) = a street: *Canongate, Eastgate.*

gil(le) *Gaelic* **gille** a boy, young man; a servant (usually referring to the servant of a saint).

glac(k) from *Gaelic* **glac** a hollow.

glas(s) from *Gaelic* **glas** grey, greenish-grey, green.

glen from *Gaelic* **gleann** a glen.

gour, gower from *Gaelic* **gabhar** a goat.

hal(l)y *Scots* form(s) of 'holy'.

haugh [hawch] *Scots* = a meadow.

heugh [hyooch] *Scots* = a cliff, precipice, steep bank.

hop(e) may be from *Old Norse* **hóp** a bay, or, especially in southern Scotland, from *Scots* **hope** an upland valley (from *Old English* **hop** a piece of enclosed land).

how(e) *Scots* = a hollow, a basin, a piece of low ground.

inch, ins(c)h from *Gaelic* **innis** a meadow; an island.

inner may be *English* **inner**, but frequently from *Gaelic* **inbhir** see **inver**.

ins(c)h see **inch**.

inver from *Gaelic* **inbhir** a rivermouth.

ken, kin from *Gaelic* **ceann** a head.

ker may be from *Gaelic* **ceathramh** a fourth part (see also **car**); or from *Old Norse* **kjarr** brushwood, a thicket.

kil from *Gaelic* **cill** a cell, church.

kin see **ken**.

knock, nock from *Gaelic* **cnoc** a hill.

know(e) *Scots* = a knoll, small hill.

kyle(s) from *Gaelic* **caolas** a (narrow) strait.

lag *Gaelic* = a hollow. **laggan** = a little hollow.

laid(e), led from *Gaelic* **leathad** a slope, hillside.

lairig *Gaelic* = a mountain pass.

land *Scots* (*in street names, especially in Edinburgh*)

= a tenement: *Gladstone's Land.*

law *Scots* = a rounded or conical hill.

lax *Old Norse* = a salmon.

leck from *Gaelic* leac a flat stone, slab.

led see **laid(e).**

les, lis from *Gaelic* lios a garden; an enclosure.

letter(s) from *Gaelic* leitir a steep hill slope.

links see Scots section.

lin(n) from *Gaelic* linne a pool or Old English *hlynh* a waterfall, torrent.

lis see **les.**

loan *Scots* = a grassy track, especially a cattle track leading to a pasture; sometimes from *Gaelic* lòn.

lon(e), loan often from *Gaelic* lòn a meadow; a marsh — but see also above.

lui from *Gaelic* laoigh of the calf.

lu(i)b from *Gaelic* lùb a bend.

machar see *Gaelic* machair.

maddy see *Gaelic* madadh.

mains *Scots* = the home farm of an estate *(common in farm names).*

mam *Gaelic* = a large rounded hill.

march *Scots* = a boundary.

mell(an), mell(on) from *Gaelic* meall a rounded hill; an, on from *Gaelic* an meaning 'of the'.

merse *Scots* = flat land along a river or estuary.

miln- *Older Scots* spelling of 'mill'.

mon(i) usually *Gaelic* monadh a hill, moor.

mont, mount may be *English* 'mount' but more frequently *Gaelic* monadh.

mo(u)nth from *Gaelic* monadh.

more from *Gaelic* mór big.

moss *Scots* = (a stretch of) moorland, boggy ground.

muck often from *Gaelic* **muc** a pig.

nes(s) *Scots* (from *Old English* or *Old Norse*) = a headland; in Shetland, Orkney and the North-West, directly from *Old Norse*; the River Ness however is an ancient river name.

nether as in *English*, lower, usually referring to the lower of two places, especially farms.

-nis(h) in *Gaelic* **nis**, from *Old Norse* **nes** — see **nes(s)** above.

nock see **knock**.

nor *Scots* = north.

ob *Gaelic* = a bay (from *Old Norse* **hóp**).

ochter see **auchter**.

ord *Gaelic* = a hammer.

our from *Gaelic* **odhar** dun-coloured, fawnish-brown.

pen *Welsh/British* a head.

pend *(in street names)* see Scots section.

penny, pin from **pennyland,** an old Scots measure of land.

pit, pet(t) from *Pictish* meaning a share, portion, a farm.

pol(l) from *Gaelic* **poll** a pool; a hole; a muddy field; or from *Norse* **bolstaðr** — see **-bost**.

-pool see **-bost**.

pres(s) from *Gaelic* **preas** a bush; a thicket.

quarrel *Scots* = a quarry.

rannoch, rannich from *Gaelic* **raineach** fern; bracken.

ree from *Gaelic* **rìgh** a king, or from **ruighe** a shieling, or from **frìth** a deer forest (see Scots section).

rhu from *Gaelic* **rubha** a headland, promontory.

rig(g) *Scots* = a ridge; in farming, a raised strip of

ploughed land between furrows.

ros(s) from *Gaelic* **ros** a promontory; or may be from *Old Norse* **hross** a horse.

roy from *Gaelic* **ruadh** red, brownish-red, red-brown.

sauchie [sawchee] *Scots* = full of, surrounded by willows.

scaur *Scots* = a steep rock, cliff or bare hill.

-set(t), -setter, -ster, -shader from *Old Norse* **setr** a house, dwelling; may also be from the closely-related *Old Norse* **saetr** a pasture; a **shieling** (see Scots section).

sgor(r), sgurr *Gaelic* = a sharp, steep rock or hill.

shee from *Gaelic* **sith** peace or **sithiche** a fairy.

shen from *Gaelic* **sean** old.

sker(ry) from *Old Norse* **sker** a rock in the sea (in *Gaelic* **sgeir**).

slack from *Old Norse* **slakki** a hollow, a valley between hills; some names may be from *Gaelic* **sloc** — see **sloc(k)** below.

slew *(only found in SW Scotland)* from *Gaelic* **sliabh** a mountain, hill.

sloc(k) from *Gaelic* **sloc(hd)** a pit, hollow.

spit(t)al(l), also **spidal, spittle** *Older Scots* = a shelter for travellers, especially in mountains.

-sta from *Old Norse* **staðr** a dwelling, a farm.

stan(e) *Scots* = a stone.

-ster see **-set(t)**.

stob *Gaelic* = a stake, pointed stick; a pointed hill.

strath from *Gaelic* **srath** a broad valley.

stron(e) often from *Gaelic* **sròn** a nose; a point of land.

stuc(k) from *Gaelic* **stuc(hd)** a small jutting hill; a peak; a cliff.

tannach, tannoch from *Old Gaelic* **tamhnach** a green and fertile field.

tar *Gaelic* = across, over.

tarbe(r)t, tarbat from *Gaelic* **tairbeart** an isthmus (literally 'across-bringing').

tarf(f) tarv from *Gaelic* **tarbh** a bull.

tay, tee, ty often from *Gaelic* **taigh** a house; the River Tay however is an ancient *Celtic* river name, meaning 'the silent one'.

temple often name of what was at one time the property of the Knights Templar.

tibber see **tober**.

tillie, tullie, tullich, tulloch from *Gaelic* **tulach** a (smallish) hill.

tipper see **tober**.

tir(e), tyre from *Gaelic* **tìr** land.

tober, tibber, tipper from *Gaelic* **tobar** a well.

tod *Scots* = a fox.

tol(l) from *Gaelic* **toll** a hole, hollow.

tom *Gaelic* = a small rounded hill.

-ton, -toun from *Old English* **tun** a farm.

tor(r), tore from *Gaelic* **tòrr** a steep conical hill.

-toul from *Gaelic* **(an) t-sabhail** of the barn.

tullie, tullich, tulloch see **tillie**.

ty see **tay**.

tyre see **tir(e)**.

-vaig see **-vik**.

-val from *Old Norse* **fjall** a hill, mountain.

vane from *Gaelic* **bhàn,** feminine etc of **bàn** fair.

vat from *Old Norse* **vatn** water, a lake.

vennel *Scots (now mainly in street names)* = a narrow street between houses.

-**vi(k)**, -**vaig**, -**vig** from *Old Norse* **vík** a bay.

-**way**, -**wall** from *Old Norse* **vágr** a bay.

weem *Scots* = a cave (from *Gaelic* **uamh**).

-**wick**, may be from *Old Norse* **vík** a bay or, in southern Scotland, from *Old English* **wic** a farm.

wynd *Scots (now mainly used in street names)* = a narrow street or lane off a main street.

yett *Scots* = a gate; a pass between hills.

SOME SCOTTISH
FIRST NAMES

(including familiar forms).

Aenas see **Angus**.

Agnes from Greek (via Latin) meaning pure, until recently a very popular girl's name in Scotland. Often shortened to **Aggie** or **Nessie**. **Senga** is the same name spelt backwards.

Aileen popular form of Eileen in Scotland; both are of Irish origin.

Ailsa girl's name, probably from Ailsa Craig, a rocky island in the Firth of Clyde.

Alasdair [alastər] *Gaelic* for Alexander. Anglicized spellings include **Alastair, Alistair, Alister** (with increasing anglicization).

Alison a diminutive form of Alice.

Angus from *Gaelic* Aonghas [oe:nəs], from an old name meaning unique choice, sometimes anglicized as **Aenas**; shortened to **Gus**.

Bella see **Isabella**.

Beth *Scots* form of Elizabeth.

Calum *Gaelic* for Malcolm; *Gaelic* **Maol Chaluim** meaning servant of Columba.

Cameron see surname list.

Campbell see surname list.

Catriona [kətreeənə] *Gaelic* for Catherine. Sometimes anglicized as **Katrina**.

Coinneach see **Kenneth**.

Colin from *Gaelic* **Cailean**.

Craig see surname list.

Deirdre name of a heroine of Irish legend who came to Scotland to escape a family quarrel.

Diarmid [dermid] name of a hero of Celtic legend, said to be the progenitor of Clan Campbell.

Donald from *Gaelic* **Dòmhnall** of Celtic origin, meaning world strength. Shortened to **Don** or **Donnie.**

Dougal, Dugald [doogəl(d)] from *Gaelic* **Dùghall** from an old name meaning black stranger, often shortened to **Doug(ie)** [doog(ee)] although, especially in the Lowlands, the latter is more commonly short for **Douglas,** which is often used as a first name; usually pronounced [dug(ee)].

Duncan a common Highland name, from *Gaelic* **Donnchadh,** from an old name meaning brown warrior.

Effie *Scots* form of Euphemia.

Eilidh [aylee] *Gaelic* for Helen.

Ella see **Isabella.**

Elspeth *Scots* form of Elizabeth.

Ewan, Ewen from *Gaelic* **Eoghann** of obscure origin.

Farquhar [farchər] from *Gaelic* **Fearchar,** from an old name meaning dear man.

Fergus from *Gaelic* **Fearchas,** from an old name meaning supremely choice.

Finlay from *Gaelic* **Fionnlagh,** from an old name meaning fair hero.

Fiona a girl's name invented by the 19th-century writer William Sharp for his pseudonym, Fiona Macleod.

Flora in Latin, a flower goddess, often used as substitute for *Gaelic* **Fionnghal** fair-shouldered.

Gavin a name of Welsh origin, in Middle English **Gawain,** it has been popular in Scotland since the Middle Ages.

Geordie *Scots* form of George.

Gordon see surname list.

Graham see surname list.

Grant see surname list.

Gus see **Angus.**

Hamish from *Gaelic* **Seumas** James. This name is an anglicized spelling of the vocative case, **a Sheumais** [ə haymish].

Hector used as a substitute for *Gaelic* **Eachann,** probably meaning horseman.

Hugh used as a substitute for Gaelic names such as **Uisdean, Aodh.**

Iain, Ian [eeən] *Gaelic* for John.

Iona girl's name from the West Coast island.

Isabella (from the same Hebrew origin as Elizabeth) has long been popular in Scotland in one form or another. **Isobel** is a distinctively *Scottish* form. *Gaelic* form is **Iseabail** [eeshəpəl], often anglicized as **Ishbel.** Pet forms include **Bella, Ella, Isa.**

Isla girl's name from the river name.

Jamie *Scots* form of James.

Janet has long been popular in Scotland along with pet forms such as **Jennie** (elsewhere for Jennifer), **Jessie** and the French-influenced form **Janette** [jənet]. *Gaelic* form is **Seònaid** [shaw:nat^y], sometimes anglicized as **Shona.**

Jean is a popular name, along with its pet form **Jeanie.**

Jock *Scots* form of John.

Katrina see **Catriona.**

Kenneth from an old *Gaelic* name **Cined,** but also used as anglicization of *Gaelic* **Coinneach** [**ki**nyach], from an old name meaning fair one. Shortened to **Ken** or **Kenny.**

Leslie (usually a boy's name), **Lesley** (girl's name) from the surname.

Lindsay a boy's or girl's name, from the surname.

Lorna a name invented by R D Blackmore for the heroine of his novel *Lorna Doone.* Popular in Scotland probably by association with the place-name **Lorn(e),** the district in Argyll, which is also used as a first name, mainly but not exclusively for boys.

Mairi [**ma:**ree] *Gaelic* for Mary; sometimes spelt **Mhairi** [**va:**ree], the vocative case in *Gaelic.*

Marsali *Gaelic* form of Marjorie.

Morag [**moa:**rək] diminutive of **Mor,** *Gaelic* for Marion.

Murdo, Murdoch from *Gaelic* **Murchadh,** from an old name meaning sea battle. The first form is a very common first name in the Highlands and the second is also a surname.

Nessie see **Agnes.**

Rab(bie), Rob(bie) *Scots* forms of Robert.

Rhona, Rona popular girl's name, perhaps connected with the two islands off the West Coast.

Roderick a Germanic name often used as a substitute for *Gaelic* **Ruaraidh.** Often shortened to **Rod(die).** See also **Rory.**

Ronald, Ranald in Scotland, probably from the Norse **Rögnvald,** meaning ruler of counsel. In *Gaelic* **Raghnall.**

Rory from *Gaelic* **Ruaraidh** (pronounced **roo** əree), meaning the red one; sometimes spelt **Ruari** but this violates Gaelic spelling rules.

Roy from *Gaelic* Ruadh red-haired; originally used mainly as a second name, as in Rob **Roy** MacGregor.

Senga see **Agnes.**

Seònaid see **Janet.**

Sheena from *Gaelic* Sìne (pronounced **shee:**nə) Jean, Jane.

Sheila from Irish **Sile** Celia, Cecilia. In Scottish *Gaelic* Silis [**shee:**lis].

Shona see **Janet.**

Tammas, Tam(mie) Scots forms of Thomas.

Una [oonə or yoonə] an old Irish name, sometimes substituted by Winifred or Agnes.

Wilma *Scots* form of Williamina.

SOME SCOTTISH
SURNAMES

THE NUMBER of Scottish surnames beginning with **Mac** or its contracted forms, **Mc**, or **M'** is striking. These are of Gaelic origin, *mac* meaning 'son of'. In English they are used for both sexes but in Gaelic only for males, the female equivalent being **Nic**, 'daughter of'. Thus:

Seumas Mac Coinnich	James MacKenzie
Anna Nic Coinnich	Anne MacKenzie

Some of the *Mac-* names commonly found in Scotland today in fact came over from Ireland in comparatively recent times, especially with the waves of Irish immigrants who came to the industrial Lowlands in the 19th and early 20th centuries. Examples of these are *McGhee* and *McLaughlin* (the usual Scottish spelling being *MacLachlan*).

The contracted forms *Mc* and *M'* are found more frequently with Irish names, though both are also used with Scottish. *M'* is however much less common than it was a generation or two ago.

For those spelt *Mac-* there is the further problem of whether the second part should have a capital letter or not. There is wide disagreement on this point, even among Gaelic speakers. One argument is that a personal name should have a capital but not, for example, a trade name: thus *MacDonald*, but *Macintyre*. Another is that since these names are in anglicized forms, there should be no capital letter in the middle of a word. The first of these has been applied in this list, but practice remains highly variable.

Quite a large number of Scottish surnames are of Norman-French origin, such as *Bruce, Cumming* (or *Comyn*), *Fraser, Grant, Hay, Lindsay, Sinclair.* They are descended from Norman-French nobles, who were granted land by the medieval kings of Scotland.

Armstrong a Border family, known for their aggressive exploits during the troubled Middle Ages.

Baxter *Older Scots* for baker.

Bruce a family of Norman-French origin, the name 'de Brus' (from Brix in Normandy) altering to become 'the Bruce' in the name of Scotland's most illustrious medieval king, Robert the Bruce.

Buchanan [bəkanən] from the family's lands on the shores of Loch Lomond.

Cameron from *Gaelic* Camshron twisted nose.

Campbell from *Gaelic* Cambeul twisted mouth.

Carnegie from the lands in Angus once owned by the family.

Chisholm [tshizəm] from the lands they once owned in Roxburghshire. Some of the family moved to the North in the 14th century, and became a Highland clan.

Colquhoun [kəhoon] from the family's lands on the shores of Loch Lomond.

Craig from *Gaelic* creag a rock.

Cumming or **Comyn** [kumin] a Norman-French name from the plant cumin. The Comyns were powerful landowners in medieval Scotland, rivalling Robert the Bruce in the early 13th century.

Cunningham from the area in the north of Ayrshire where they owned lands.

Dalziel, Dalyell [dee-el] from the district of that name in Lanarkshire.

Douglas from the river-name, meaning black stream. The Douglases were one of the most powerful families in medieval Scotland.

Drummond from Drymen near Loch Lomond, although the family lands were later further east in Perthshire.

Forbes [formerly pronounced **for**bis, now usually forbz] from the lands in the valley of the Don in Aberdeenshire.

Fraser or **Frazer** a Norman-French name, their ancestor came to Scotland in the 12th century.

Gilchrist [**gil**krist] from *Gaelic* **Gille-Crìosd** servant of Christ.

Gillespie [gi**lespee**] from *Gaelic* **Gill-easbuig** bishop's servant.

Gillies [**gil**is] from *Gaelic* **Gille Iosa** servant of Jesus.

Gordon from the lands in Berwickshire which the family originally held; they were later granted territory in the North-East by Robert the Bruce.

Gow from *Gaelic* **gobha** a smith.

Graham their ancestor was an Anglo-Norman noble, the name of whose English manor meant grey home.

Grant a Norman-French name from French 'le Grand' the big one.

Hay a Norman-French name from La Haye in Normandy.

Innes from the coastal area in Moray.

Leslie from the area in Aberdeenshire.

Lindsay an Anglo-Norman family, the name coming from Lindsey, meaning island of the lime tree, in Northern England.

MacBeth from *Gaelic* **Mac Bheatha** son of life.

MacInnes from *Gaelic* **Mac Aonghuis** son of Angus.

Macintyre from *Gaelic* **Mac an t-saoir** son of the carpenter.

MacKay from *Gaelic* **Mac Aoidh,** son of **Aodh,** an old Gaelic name, sometimes anglicized as Hugh.

MacKenzie from *Gaelic* **Mac Coinnich** son of **Coinneach** an old Gaelic name anglicized as **Kenneth.** Formerly pronounced [məkingee] — for the 'z' in spelling, see Introduction.

MacKinnon from *Gaelic* **Mac Fionnghain,** son of **Fingan.**

Mackintosh from *Gaelic* **Mac an Tòisich,** son of the toiseach or chief.

MacLaren, MacLaurin from *Gaelic* **Mac Labhruinn** son of Laurence.

Maclean [məklayn] from *Gaelic* **Mac Gill-Eathain** son of the servant of John.

MacLeod [məklowd] from *Gaelic* **Mac Leòid** son of Leod, a 13th-century Norse ancestor (*Norse* **Ljótr** ugly).

Macpherson from *Gaelic* **Mac a' Phearsoin** son of the parson.

Mactaggart from *Gaelic* **Mac an t-Sagairt** son of the priest.

MacTavish from *Gaelic* **Mac Thàmhais** son of Tammas, Scots form of Thomas.

Menzies a Norman-French name (from Mesnières in

Normandy), now usually pronounced as it is spelt, but
Scottish pronunciation is [**meeng**is] or [**ming**is].

Mor(r)ison son of Morris, but used in the Highlands
and Islands as an anglicization of *Gaelic*, either **Mac
Ghille Mhoire,** son of the servant of Mary, or
O Muirgheasàin, name of an Irish family who became
hereditary poets to Scottish clan chiefs. In modern
Gaelic, **Moireasdan.**

Murray from Moray in North-East Scotland.

Ogg from *Gaelic* òg young.

Ogilvie from the lands in Angus.

Ross from the Northern county.

Sinclair a Norman-French name from Saint-Clair-sur-
Elle in Normandy.

Stewart ancestors of some Stewarts were hereditary
Stewards of Scotland, an important office at the
medieval Scottish court. Through the marriage of
Walter the Steward to Marjorie, daughter of King
Robert the Bruce, Scotland, and later of Great Britain,
acquired a line of Stewart monarchs. The spelling
Stuart, latterly used by the royal house, is due to
French influence at the time of Mary, Queen of Scots.

Sutherland from the area in the extreme north-west of
Scotland (which was nevertheless 'south-land' to the
Norsemen).

Urquhart [**ur**chart] from the place-name in Inverness-
shire.

Wallace means Welsh, probably referring to the British
inhabitants of Strathclyde, what is now South-West
Scotland.

Webster *Older Scots* for weaver.

FOOD AND DRINK

SCOTTISH food at its wholesome best can be of very high quality. Some of the natural ingredients produced in this small and seemingly unfavourable part of the world are unsurpassed anywhere. The meat, especially hill lamb and beef, is prized the world over, as is Scottish trout and salmon, now, thanks to fish farms, more widely available. Game birds abound, especially grouse and pheasant, and Scotland does not sufficiently appreciate the venison from the large red-deer population, as a high proportion of it is exported to Europe.

Certain parts of Scotland produce excellent soft fruits, especially raspberries in the Dundee-Perth area, but also strawberries, for example in the Upper Clyde valley. Wild raspberries are one of the pleasures of the countryside, as are blackberries, known here as brambles, in the autumn.

Perhaps the food most associated with Scotland is oats, a cereal crop which tends to be despised elsewhere. Dr Johnson's definition — 'a food which in England is generally given to horses, but in Scotland supports the people' — may still be regarded as valid by a few, but its food value is now much more appreciated. Everyone has heard of porridge, oatcakes and haggis, but there are numerous other dishes of which it is the main ingredient; the following is a small selection of these:

Athole brose a mixture of honey, oatmeal, whisky and water.
bannock a round flat cake, usually made of oatmeal, but thicker and softer than an oatcake.

brose oatmeal mixed with boiling water or milk, with salt, butter etc added. Special varieties are also eaten, especially in the North-East, such as **neep brose,** made with water in which turnips have been cooked.

crannachan a dessert of whipped cream, toasted oatmeal etc.

mealie pudding a kind of sausage made of oatmeal, suet, onions, seasoning.

skirlie similar ingredients fried.

Scots housewives have long been known for their skill in baking and a large variety of cakes and other baking can also be found in shops throughout the country. The names of some of these examples have to be distinguished from their English (or American) counterparts.

sweet

black bun or **Scotch bun** a very rich spicy fruit cake, baked in a pastry case, eaten at New Year.

cookie a round, light, sweet, dark-glazed bun, made with a yeast dough; often filled with whipped cream (**cream cookie**).

Dundee cake a rich fruit cake with almonds on top.

French cake a small oblong sponge cake covered with icing.

Selkirk bannock a rich fruit loaf.

shortbread a kind of crisp crumbly biscuit made of flour, butter and sugar, traditional fare at New Year.

less sweet

Abernethy biscuit a kind of large, light crisp biscuit.

crumpet a very thin largish **pancake** (see below), often rolled up with jam etc inside.

muffin a small round thick **scone**.

oatcake a crisp biscuit made of oatmeal and water with a little salt and fat.

pancake or **dropped scone** a small round flat cake baked by dropping a very soft dough onto a **girdle** etc.

parkin a kind of spiced biscuit made of oatmeal, flour, treacle etc.

potato scone or **tattie scone** a thin flat cake made of mashed potatoes, flour, butter and salt.

scone a semi-sweet cake made of a soft dough and baked either on a **girdle** etc or in the oven, usually in a large round cut into triangular sections.

There is also a great variety of sweets, or sweeties, such as:

black man a kind of dark-coloured candy or toffee, made with treacle.

black strippit ba a hard, round, peppermint-flavoured sweet with black and white stripes.

boiling a boiled sweet.

cheugh Jeans or **teuch Jeans** [tshuch] a kind of very chewy toffee.

Edinburgh rock a light, stick-shaped sweet made of sugar, water and cream of tartar, with flavouring and pastel colouring.

Hawick ball a hard cinnamon or mint-flavoured sweet, made in Hawick.

Jeddart snail a kind of dark toffee, made in Jedburgh.

oddfellow a small pastel-coloured sweet, flavoured with cinnamon etc.

pan drop a round white peppermint sweet, a mint imperial.

soor ploom a tart-flavoured round green boiled sweet.

tablet a kind of fudge, of a hard consistency.

Scotland's national drink is usually considered to be whisky, although its history as a prestige drink does not go as far back as one might imagine. The favoured drink of the upper classes in the past was claret and the wine trade between Edinburgh (or rather Leith) and Bordeaux from the early Middle Ages has been well documented. Today however whisky is one of our chief exports and much of it is drunk by all classes at home — for good and ill.

Whisky is sometimes known as barley bree, but the name is appropriate only to one of the two types of whisky produced — **malt whisky,** which is distilled from malted barley only. This is the more refined drink and is produced by a very large number of manufacturers whose resounding names — Glenlivet, Glenfiddich, Glenmorangie — may be seen in profusion around the shelves of many Scottish bars. The more ordinary drink is **blended whisky,** made from a mixture of malt whisky and whisky made from grain (usually maize). Some blends, such as Chivas Regal, the Antiquary, are given additional flavour, prestige — and price — by a higher proportion of malt to grain.

Beer is also drunk in large quantities in Scotland and its terminology differs from that south of the Border:

    heavy approximately as English bitter.
    export a slightly stronger and darker-coloured beer than heavy.
    light a low-gravity beer.
    special a carbonated version of heavy.
    pale ale a low-gravity beer.

The real ale movement has had some success in Scotland and has led to the re-introduction of an old Scottish classification of beer strength, based on the price per barrel, eg 70/- (70 shilling) ale, a beer of medium strength.

Book list and further information
SCOTS LANGUAGE

General

A J Aitken, Tom McArthur eds *Languages of Scotland* 1979; 160 pp; a collection of essays on Scots and Gaelic.

Aonghus MacNeacail and Iseabail Macleod *Scotland a Linguistic Double Helix* 1995; booklet on Gaelic and Scots from the European Bureau for Lesser Used Languages.

Dictionaries

Scottish National Dictionary 1931-76; 10 vols; the Scots language from 1700 to the present time.

Dictionary of the Older Scottish Tongue 1931-; now published to S; the Scots language up to 1700.

Concise Scots Dictionary 1985; 862 pp; one-volume reduced version of both the above.

Scots Super-mini Dictionary 1988, 1997; 360 pp, pocket Scots-English Dictionary.

Concise English-Scots Dictionary 1993; 302 pp.

General

Two small books giving an account of the language, its history and its present position:

J Derrick McClure *Why Scots matters* 1988, 1997.

David Murison *The Guid Scots Tongue* 1977.

For further information:

Scottish National Dictionary Association,
27 George Square, Edinburgh EH8 9LD
Tel and Fax 0131-650 4149
email: mail@snda.org.uk.

Scots Language Resource Centre
A K Bell Library
York Place, Perth
Tel 01738 440199   fax 01738 477010

GAELIC

Dictionaries

Robert C Owen *The Modern Gaelic-English Dictionary* 1993, 139 pp.

Derick S Thomson *The New English-Gaelic Dictionary* 1981, 210 pp.

Abair Facail 1979, small Gaelic-English/English-Gaelic Dictionary for learners (short word list but good grammatical information).

Edward Dwelly *The Illustrated Gaelic-English Dictionary* 1911, 1034 pp, a remarkably comprehensive dictionary written by an Englishman at the end of the last century, packed with interesting information but not easy for the learner to use.

Alexander MacBain *An Etymological Dictionary of the Gaelic Language* 1911, useful information on word origins.

General

Kenneth MacKinnon *Gaelic a Past and Future Prospect* 1991, 208 pp.

Derick S Thomson ed *A Companion to Gaelic Culture* 1983, 1994, 363 pp.

Courses

Speaking our Language 1993-4; television course with study packs, audio, video etc.

Hugo Scottish Gaelic in Three Months 1996.

Teach Yourself Gaelic 1993 book and cassette.

Can Seo Gaelic for Beginners 1979, 128 pp, the course book for a Gaelic course on BBC television.

For further information:

Comunn na Gàidhlig, 5 Mitchells Lane, Inverness IV2 3HQ. tel 01463 234138   fax 01463 237470

Comann an Luchd-Ionnsachaidh, (Gaelic Learners' Association), 62 High Street, Invergordon IV18 0LQ. tel and fax 01349 854848

PLACE-NAMES

W F Nicolisen *Scottish Place-names* 1976, 210 pp. a descriptive study rather than a reference book.

J B Johnston *The Place-names of Scotland* 1903, 308 pp.

J B Johnston, *Gazetteer of Scotland*, 1937, 1973, 353 pp.

W J Watson, *The History of Celtic Place-names of Scotland* 1926, 1986, 576 pp, a standard work on an important aspect of Scottish place-names.

Alexander MacBain *Place-names Highlands and Islands of Scotland* 1922, 381 pp.

W C Mackenzie *Scottish Place-names* 1931, 320 pp.

Place-names on maps of Scotland and Wales 1973, 233 pp, an Ordnance Survey guide which includes Gaelic and Scandinavian elements.

David Dorward *Scotland's Place-names* 1995, 176 pp, an introduction to place-name elements.

Iain Taylor *Scottish Place-names* 1997, 160 pp.

For mountain names, *Munro's Tables*, edited by Derek A Bearhop, 1997, contains an appendix with translations of names of Munros and Corbetts.

Peter Drummond *Scottish Hill and Mountain Names* 1992, 184 pp.

Regional books include:
Hugh Marwick *Orkney Farm Names* 1952

Adam Watson and Elizabeth Allan *The Place Names of Upper Deeside* 1984, 192 pp, an in-depth study of a small part of Aberdeenshire.

W J Watson *Place-names of Ross and Cromarty* 1904, 302 pp, a detailed study of Ross-shire names.
William M Alexander *The Place-names of Aberdeenshire* 1952.

Further information from:
Place-name Survey, School of Scottish Studies, 27 George Square, Edinburgh EH8 9LD.

PERSONAL NAMES

George F Black *The Surnames of Scotland* 1946, 838 pp.

Leslie Alan Dunkling *Scottish Christian Names* 1978, 154 pp.

David Dorward, *Scottish Surnames* 1994, 384 pp.

FOOD AND DRINK

Cookery books

Catherine Brown Scottish Cookery 1985, 304 pp, interesting book to browse through as well as a recipe book.

Catherine Brown *Scottish Regional Recipes* 1981.

Catherine Brown *A Year in the Scots Kitchen* 1996, 194 pp.

Theodora Fitzgibbon *A Taste of Scotland* 1970.

F Marian MacNeill *The Scots Kitchen Its Lore and Recipes* 1929, 260 pp, once a standard work but now rather dated.

Scottish Women's Rural Institutes Cookery Book (8th Edition) 208 pp.

The Glasgow Cookery Book (4th Edition) 1975.

General

Catherine Brown *From Broth to Bannocks* 1990, 273 pp, a history of Scottish food and cooking from the seventeenth century.

G W Lockhart *The Scot and His Oats* 1983, 57 pp, the story of the oat crop and its uses.

Maisie Steven T*he Good Scots Diet– What Happened to it?* 1985, 185 pp, a dietician's view of Scottish food past and present

Drink

Derek Cooper *Companion to Whiskies* 1983, 170 pp.

David Daiches *Scotch Whisky Past and Present* 1969, 176 pp.

Neil M Gunn *Whisky and Scotland* 1935, 198 pp, whisky and its history and the novelist's views on both.

Billy Kay and Cailean Maclean *Knee Deep in Claret* 1983, 232 pp, (casting doubt on what really is Scotland's national drink!)